DEDICATION

To:

My Almighty God, for the wonderful gift of life and grace

My beloved mother, who is sadly no longer now, for her wisdoms

My beautiful wife and best friend, Elisa, for your boundless support and kindness, and to our adorable son and daughter, Nathanael and Odilie, for your unconditional love and endless laughter.

All of you, Les Brown, Robert Kiyosaki, Tony Robbins, Russell Brunson, Bob Proctor, Lisa Nichols, Stephen Larsen and Julie Stoian for your priceless teachings and inspiration

And to you, readers of this book, I'd like to thank you and urge you to let your inner greatness shine and inspire others!

PREFACE

Could this be your AHAAA moment as well?

Married to the best wife in this world and father of two adorable children, all I wanted, following my graduation from the University of Manchester in the United Kingdom, a few years back, was that my beautiful wife and our loving children should always feel that I can provide for them, that I can protect them no matter what, that I have it all figured out and that I have everything under control! Sound familiar?

To achieve that, I had my plans and worked for banking and telecommunication corporations. But after being made redundant twice, it was time to rethink my strategies!

I developed and managed up to 15 businesses in the last 10 years, online and offline. I did well with some of them for a short period of time. Eventually, I had enough of trading my time for money!

I then decided to explore entrepreneurial opportunities. I started looking for the best system and products to use to generate a steady passive income and be able to attain financial, location and temporal freedom! I invested extensively in learning various systems and products, but I could not get what I wanted.

*Then I had my **epiphany moment** or my **Ahaaaa moment** as I finally discovered what I was looking for. My journey has allowed me to experience unprecedented personal transformation and entrepreneurial growth. Therefore, I could not help but invest all I could to write this indispensable book that has turned out to be a must have tool to help start-up entrepreneurs and advanced marketers develop and scale their businesses to success.*

The Life You Want; The Marriage You Want... The Family That You Want, Is Going To Be Fueled By The Business You Build... (*Russell Brunson*)

For whom much has been given, a lot is also required! I hope this piece of work will also help someone out there! Could it be you?

If this book helps you in any way, may I ask you to leave a helpful review on our *Amazon book page "How To Improve Conversions, Sales And Profits - by Kalombe Andy Mutambya"* and your supportive comment on our *Facebook page "Recurring Income Ideas"*. You are also entitled to join our *Facebook Group "Highest Paying Affiliate Program"* to be able to share and learn more from other entrepreneurs on a continual basis.

! Websites Are Dead !

Top 7 Weird Secrets to Increase Your Traffic, Conversions and Sales

Unlock and Leverage New Powers of Internet, Turning Ordinary Entrepreneurs into Super Money-Making Machines!

Powerful Steps to Help You Skyrocket Your Passive Income

Table of Contents

DEDICATION 1

PREFACE 2

INTRODUCTION 6

SECRET 1: WHAT ARE THE 4 MUSTS ALL SUPER ONLINE ENTREPRENEURS HAVE IN COMMON? 9

SECRET 2: WHY THE 'WHO' AND NOT THE 'HOW'?...19

SECRET 4: WHY AND HOW MUST YOU HACK YOUR INFLUENCER?.......................................45

SECRET 5: WHY AND HOW MUST YOU BE NOISY AND CREATE MASS MOVEMENT? 65

SECRET 6: WHY IS COLLEGE TEACHING IRRELEVANT IN TODAY'S MARKET FOR ENTREPRENEURS? 77

SECRET 7: WHAT IS THAT VEHICLE OR PLATFORM THAT WILL TURN YOU INTO THAT MONEY-MAKING MACHINE? 80

CONCLUSION 93

Introduction

Passive income business opportunities are increasingly recognized as obvious ways to make a living online. Regrettably, websites, as we have known them, are not converting as they use to. Are websites dead?

But how are ordinary entrepreneurs suddenly turning into super money-making machines? They have discovered the secrets!

Should there be any reason why traditional websites are dead today? A large number of online entrepreneurs and marketers are yet to discover, unlock and leverage new powers of internet, which are turning ordinary entrepreneurs into super money-making machines! This is obviously the reason why many passive income business models are not doing well or are completely dead.

There are secrets to discover in order to make it big online as an entrepreneur. It is up to you to find them out. As a marketer or an online entrepreneur, starting out is the first step you have to take to embrace your passive income journey.

You're now on your journey. So, if your goal for starting an online business is to make profits and earn a living for yourself, then steps towards increasing your traffic, optimizing your conversions and boosting your sales should be the driving force to keep you going.

Are you highly motivated? Perhaps you simply don't know what to do right now to get your online business to a peak. What does it take to increase sales as a digital marketer? The plain truth is, you're a product of the information you have stored in you. If you know the secrets to driving traffic to your business, boosting conversions and ultimately increasing sales, it's not hard to make your passive income business generate big profits.

Not everyone knows how things work over the internet when it comes to digital marketing, online entrepreneurship and earning good income with a passive income business idea. It is hoped that with this book you will get your business going the right way. If you desire to learn and understand why things are working the way they are or why you should be acting differently to achieve better results, you can rest assured to find what you require right in here.

This book highlights the critical issues why websites are dead, while shedding the light on the top 7 weird secrets being used by all the top entrepreneurs in order to help increase traffic, conversions and sales. Online entrepreneurs will discover the top 7 weird secrets and be able to boost their online income. Digital marketers wishing to drive sufficient traffic to their products and services, improve conversions and increase sales will find the content of this book greatly useful in growing their online business.

Have you had enough of your current situation? Can you commit to your commitment? It is time you follow and implement these powerful steps designed to help you skyrocket your passive income to a greater height. Don't sit on the fence. "Not being able to decide is a decision – Don't die with your music in you."

Many people are getting lost through processes learned in school, including outdated business plan concepts, debt and many other aspects that make starting a business seem impossible for an ordinary person. This situation leads the majority of entrepreneurs to a lack of belief, endless procrastination and frustration, keeping them in the rat race, doing the jobs they hate and an overall unfulfilled life.

The following money-making secrets are in line with human psychology and are applicable to all types of industries. Therefore, whether you are selling products or services online or offline, at very high prices or low-tickets, these awesome secrets will take you and your business to the highest level!

Secret 1: What Are The 4 Musts All Super Online Entrepreneurs Have In Common?

Clearly speaking, traditional websites are dead, but some smart online entrepreneurs and direct marketing business men and women are still able to rise above the waters to withstand the tides and make great impact with their businesses. They surely are doing some things right and differently to still turn out good profits in their endeavors online. And they are not leaving anything to chance. Want to skyrocket your passive income business like theirs? Model your online business like theirs and you'll surely get similar results if not better. These four must-have values are obligatory for your success. Imbibe them in your life and give a lift to your business.

To skyrocket your passive income and join the winning smart entrepreneurs club, these four must-have principles are a powerful source of inspiration:

1.   *Belief*
2.   *Willingness to Unlearn*
3.   *Willingness to Re-learn*
4.   *Focus*

Get hold of these top sets of weird secrets and enjoy the start of magic increase of your business traffic, conversions and sales.

Why Belief, Willingness to Unlearn, to Re-learn and Focus are the driving forces to help you jumpstart or grow your business to its peak while turning you into that online money-making machine you so desire?

First, you need to work on yourself. These four vital principles are designed to help you do that. Let's take a look at how each works to shape your mind and help your business grow.

Belief:

Many websites are dead right at their launch because marketers and entrepreneurs fail on the matter of belief. Without belief, you cannot get anything done or even be ambitious as a digital marketer or as an online entrepreneur. You've got to believe in yourself that you can do it! Ordinary online entrepreneurs turned online money-making machines rely on the belief in their abilities and potential. "It is done unto you according to your belief," says my Loving Father!

Some individuals claim that it is your background, luck, resources or connections that make you successful. I beg to differ. While I surely agree that all these and many other factors may affect each individual's path, self-belief is the most important factor in reaching your goals. There isn't much that could help you reach your objectives without this important ingredient.

James Clear once said that the greatest distinction he's noticed is not intelligence or chance or resources between successful and unsuccessful individuals. It's the conviction or the belief they carry in them to accomplish what they are set to do. Self-belief is just about everything, it's the starting point to business success. Therefore, work on yourself!

If you don't trust yourself, who else will? If belief is missing, your websites are dead as a result and cannot serve their purpose. Don't ignore!

Honestly, if you don't think you'll succeed, how would anyone else do that for you? Let's say you are starting up a great company, and you need to persuade investors that your concept is worth financing.

The first thing is to believe that your business idea will succeed; otherwise, no one else will. As an online entrepreneur, you must first of all equip yourself with unshakable belief which is part of the first sets of the top 7 secrets to increase traffic, conversions and boost sales. The rest of the work becomes easier afterward.

Imagine a life without your arms and legs. That's Nick Vujicic's story. Everybody doubted his capacity to live a normal life, including himself! He even tried to commit suicide. However, the turning point came when he discovered faith and the power that comes along with it.

Now, Nick lives a life without constraints, traveling the globe and inspiring millions of individuals to live limitless life based on belief, regardless of his own disabilities.

You need to realize that your brain is always playing tricks against you on the path to success. Your big goals in you don't matter; the only thing your brain is more interested in is to keep you alive. That's why it gives way to procrastination, negative thoughts, self-doubt, and anxiety, among others. These are nothing but false belief! The sure way to overcome these barriers is not to believe in them and to keep thinking positively. The road to success in your entrepreneurial journey should start off from believing in yourself.

Self-belief:

- Helps to build self-confidence

- Takes you steps closer to achieving your dream and making a success out of your endeavor.

- Inspires you to take action

- Gives you the right and positive attitude you need for success

- Helps you overcome the negative thoughts

- Makes you see failure as part of your success journey

Learn:

Shocked why your business websites are dead?

Want to unlock and leverage new powers of internet turning ordinary entrepreneurs into super money-making machine? Learn and keep learning the right way! Knowledge and appropriate action are what will separate you from novices and turn you into an expert. Online entrepreneurs who know their worth don't stop learning, which includes unlearning and re-learning. So should you to keep your passive income business on the high.

Be humble to unlearn and willing to re-learn the money-making pattern untaught in school. Learning is a continuous process of life that should be done right.

Alvin Toffler puts it this way:

Twenty-first-century illiterates won't be those who can't write but those individuals who can't unlearn, learn and relearn. You can't give a spark to your passive income and increase your sales if you keep on doing things the same way as before while hoping for new results. No! That won't happen! Smart online entrepreneurs go with what works now to get today's results. They do not use dead websites to carry out their businesses but have discovered great ways of leveraging the new powers of internet to resolve problems and better serve their customers.

Learning has three phases to it: learn, unlearn and relearn. Do away with the old, unlearn out of date and unproductive methods. Learn what works today. Learn the right way by relearning what you think you already know. As an online entrepreneur, you should learn the secrets smart entrepreneurs are using. To skyrocket your passive income business, you cannot stick to the old ways of doing things! Old methods will give you the same results and you don't want that!

Learn today's ways on:

- What to do to increase traffic

- How to best increase conversions?

- The best approach to increase sales

- Discover effective passive income models

Learning cannot be referred to as simply bringing together some bits of information to enhance our experience; it also embodies unlearning and relearning. Needless to say, learning is linked to making a change. If individuals understand why they are requested to create something different, they'll be more willing to give up (unlearn) ancient techniques and embrace fresh ones (Relearn).

While we are all born with a desire to learn, many are losing their passion for learning somewhere along the line. You must make continuous learning a unique part of your entrepreneurial journey. Go along with the latest trends on how things work around the internet. Learn about what your competitors and influencers are doing right and model your business and tactics after them.

Why do many stop learning?

Whatever the reasons, when the basics are covered, many people tend to stick to whatever they know and they avoid the challenges of learning something new. Today's websites are dead because online entrepreneurs fail to keep up the learning process of unlearning and relearning all the time. You can't take this fact away from the main reasons why websites are dead today. The lack of appropriate learning is negatively impacting passive income businesses.

Don't get stuck doing the same things over and over again while expecting a different result. That won't happen. Unlearn all those concepts that have only succeeded in killing your business and caging you.

We are familiar with the word learning but perhaps not so much with the concept of unlearning and relearning. Yet, they make up the complete learning process and you must absorb that in your business if you want to increase your traffic, skyrocket your conversions and boost your sales.

Lao Tzu said in order to gain knowledge or understanding; add value to yourself every day. To achieve wisdom, remove stuff every day. One of the abilities we all need to create is learning to let go of false beliefs, ancient and outdated convictions and ideas. Online and direct marketing entrepreneurs must practice this on a regular basis in order to be able to skyrocket their businesses in today economy.

We need to unlearn practices that hold us back in numerous circumstances and get them overrun by those that enable us to achieve the desired end.

Unlearning, however, is not just about giving away a previous knowledge; it is about dismissing a previously held faith or a long-revered concept that needs to be handled with caution as it may pose a danger to the learner.

Your view about learning can be what is standing in your way in making good progress to skyrocket your passive income. Your passive income websites are dead the moment you stop learning.

For example, in the face of the slightest adversity, if students believe that learning is a matter of natural ability rather than effort, they are unlikely to try harder, to think smarter and outside the box. There must be commitment!

Bill Clinton proclaimed in 1992 that if you work hard enough and follow the rules you're going to get ahead, have a nice life and pave the way for your children to have a better one too. This is a normal statement.

Unfortunately, this isn't always true anymore! Few individuals used email before the internet began in the early 1990s, and learners continued to use encyclopedias for study tasks. It was a world where technology had little impact; a world where remote work was still a rare occurrence and many individuals were comfortable working in a single organization all through their career.

Things are no longer the same, many folks are even prepared to bend the rules to get ahead! This involves constantly questioning hypotheses about how things work, challenging ancient paradigms, and 'relearning' what's important now in your online business.

In an industry where rules change rapidly, online entrepreneurs' capability to be swift is crucial in letting go of ancient guidelines and learning fresh ones. Learning agility is the key to unlocking your ability to change and to succeed in a life that is unpredictable and constantly changing, both personally and professionally.

In your marketing drive to increase sales in your business, there are numerous concepts and practices you may have to unlearn, such as:

- Unlearning the models that you are using that are not yielding result
- Unlearning your methodology
- Unlearning how to approach your brand
- Unlearning how your value is communicated
- Unlearning the manner your value is delivered
- Unlearning who your target market is, what they want and why

Unlearning is about giving up rather than obtaining something. Add unlearning to your learning process and then relearn. This is one of the sets of main secrets to increase sales and skyrocket your passive income.

Focus:

Are your passive income businesses where you want them?

Focus is one of the powerful sets of secrets to help you skyrocket your passive income and place you in the esteemed position of great entrepreneurs of our time.

One of the main reasons why most websites are dead is that online entrepreneurs lose focus. You can't increase conversions in your passive income if 'focus' is missing. What business model are you running? Are you a marketer? What is your industry? Focus prevents you from chasing shadows.

This is one of the biggest challenges online entrepreneurs face; staying focused in the rapidly-paced, technology-driven globe in which we live. We contend with too much information and many issues in our business lives. But remaining focused is key in order to reach our goals in life and business.

Now, how do you get your eyes fixed on what matters and not everything that comes your way as an online entrepreneur?

Get your focus on one thing.

- Choose and stay with your niche. Don't try to be everywhere and do everything
- Research more on your competitors' approach to your chosen niche
- Be consistent with your platform and implementation

He who chases two birds does not catch any! Wise words from a wise person, but most people will opt to chase perhaps a dozen rabbits and a few elephants at the same moment! But if we follow Confucius ' wise words, we'll get more done and speedily accomplish our objectives.

If you spend your precious time working on more than one thing at a given time, it requires your brain time to re-adjust and focus on the second assignment when you move from one to another, and precious time is wasted in the transition. The truth is, multitasking is a nightmare of efficiency. Cut this down drastically, if you must at all.

Eliminate known distractions

Distraction is an attack on focus, and this is a big contributor to the death of websites. Your mind must settle on what you do. Disconnect from technology if you need to get the job done. Turn off all email, tweet notifications and reminders. Take control of all communications and social media and go to them only when you are willing to spend time there. You can't get to the online money-making machine status in your passive income push with all of these competing for your precious time!

Calm the mind

The greatest distraction is not as you might have assumed, social media platforms, all the time. Your mind is one. When you're attempting to get things done, it's your own ideas that will keep racing through your minds. These cheeky voices often tempt you away from the work that requires to be done, or they tell you annoyingly and repeatedly that assignment B and D stay incomplete while you are still working on assignment A. Meditation is a wonderful way to keep the mind still. It can assist to silence worries from time to time. Being able to control your mind and keeping calm will help you remain focused, boost your passive income and make you one of the top entrepreneurs in the world.

De-clutter

Surely, you intend to skyrocket your passive income, don't you? Then, go ahead and de-clutter.

Decluttering is an important step to help you remove distractions and keep focus. It covers every aspect of you. If your office desk and mind are clear, you minimize distraction chances. I always end my week by tidying and organizing my desk and anything that's been left lying around during the week. By the beginning of the following week, I'd make sure that there's nothing from the previous week that was forgotten or left undone. By getting into the habit of doing a weekly de-cluttering, it lets me start the week relaxed, focused and ready for action.

Now you know it! These four essentials make up the first main set of top 7 secrets which are imperative to skyrocket your passive income. Get more insights and further help from the Author's recommended website: www.andymutambya.com

Secret 2: Why The 'Who' And Not The 'How'?

Most of today's websites are dead on arrival and do not fulfil their purpose because the owners tend to do everything by themselves! Stop asking how you're going to get a task done in your business, look for who does it better instead and pay for it. It is more cost effective and improves productivity that way.

In this era of readily available information, it is very tempting to look for a quick fix rather than finding the appropriate "who" capable of delivering the best service. Many online entrepreneurs have that instinct. They tend to want to know how to do everything. Smart online entrepreneurs take a different approach to this. They look for the Who instead and free themselves of unnecessary burdens.

The 'Who can do it' and not the 'How to do it' should be your choice on how to get a task done. This is one of the top 7 weird secrets to increase your traffic, conversions, and sales. Putting so much effort into the "how" has led to most websites' premature death.

It is not the 'How' but the 'who' that you should set your mind on, in order to get your passive income business onto the fast track. Don't go doing everything all alone, you should outsource some other tasks to the experts.

Many online entrepreneurs get stuck, lose focus and start procrastinating when trying to figure out how to do everything by themselves. By spending half a day trying to learn to design a logo, may feel like a heavy burden compared to logo designers doing it themselves, consequently saving you time. We've all heard that time is money; you may, therefore, be leaving some on the table if you waste most of your time trying to figure out everything.

Learn how to put value on your time, then find those who are already experts in their professions and be willing to pay them for their products and services which, in turn, allows you to maintain your focus on developing and growing your business.

Know that the "Who" will Solve the "How". So look out for the WHO.

Many online entrepreneurs have excellent skills, but they often believe they can do it all, "says Sparks." That really can stop business development and hamper productivity. It is an obvious fact that justifies the reason why many websites are dead!

One of the most important values the internet has added to how businesses are better run today is the ability to outsource tasks. Most of the time, it is advised to outsource less important tasks which are time consuming. How about outsourcing as many tasks as you can if you have experts around you who can deliver better results? It surely pays dividends, doesn't it?

Online entrepreneurs have more time to concentrate on revenue generating activities by outsourcing some of their tasks. Knowing how to get things done is good but is often not always profitable, don't fall for it! You don't need to be a guru or a hero to run your business! Overburdening yourself with duties doesn't help your productivity. Find the expert and delegate.

More modest companies are outsourcing duties these days since technology has progressed to the stage where professionals can operate from around the globe, combined with the availability and accessibility of highly skilled experts who have decided to leave the corporate environment to work remotely or as freelancers such as virtual assistants, marketing managers, graphic designers, and the likes.

These freelancers come on board as subcontractors and save online entrepreneurs valuable time and money. Taking the very first steps towards outsourcing and finding adequate workforce can also be energy-consuming though, but it always turns out to be well worth it whenever you find the right fit.

Progressive online entrepreneurs understand this unstoppable secret of outsourcing which helps them manage vital elements of their companies.

The appropriate time for outsourcing is distinct for each business; know when the time is right for your business. For effective results, you should always make a plan for your outsourcing needs well in advance. The bottom line is, you should account for it as a significant part of your business!

Websites are dead for many reasons.

It is high time to consider outsourcing if you and your present staff are unable to handle your company's day-to-day business. Even if you can, searching for the "who" to resolve the "how" usually turns out to be more beneficial in the long run.

Still not sure about your need for outsourcing; here are helpful tips for you:

5 Motivations to Quit Doing Everything Individually

1. Ease your burden. As a new online entrepreneur, it's normal to feel the need of taking on more than a considerable amount of obligations. You could be clearly fit for such a task; however, it can be overwhelming and burdensome! Outsourcing will save you from this; it takes the stress off you.

2. Helps you to try out different styles easily. Variety is described as a spice of life. There is an obvious reason for that! Many people like colorful and new things. When you discover the benefits of hiring experts and how they provide a different style, you will be amazed at how quickly your business can improve. This allows you to focus on maintaining your business and managing your passive income source more efficiently. In order words, outsourcing exposes you to different ways of doing things and being flexible.

3. The job gets done even if you don't know how. When you hire someone, who is an expert in something you are struggling with, you're empowering that person while owning the gains from that collaboration. As a result, your business followers are better served, perhaps with a quality post or a lovely design and they give you all the credit for the work.

4. Lower your feelings of anxiety. You get nervous whenever you have so much to handle. Requesting help lessens pressure and makes others associate with you more while helping you build a great network for yourself. Outsourcing lets you feel relaxed and calm.

5. Saves you lots of time. When you hire an individual who likes to do what they do, you can rest assured that your work is well under control, handled accurately and with care. This leaves you a lot more time than you had when you were troubled and probably thought you needed more time to do it all yourself.

Find and hire that suitable 'who' for every aspect of your business and skyrocket your passive income. Many online entrepreneurs' websites are dead for not outsourcing correctly or not at all!

More Reasons why your business should consider outsourcing:

- Access to Tools: Outsourcing can provide access to tools that your organization would otherwise not have had access to.

- Outsourcing non-core tasks will allow you to pay more attention to those that matter most and generate the most income

- Transfer of roles: Once a job is outsourced, your organization has one less thing to worry about

- Access to knowledge and expertise: Better outcome is achieved when responsibility is passed on to professionals in a specific sector

- Capacity management: Instead of being overwhelmed by the requirements of several elements of the company, your organization can use its key employees to the optimum

- Focus on key things: If you outsource duties that include your area of weakness, you can, therefore allow yourself to concentrate on your strong points and key procedures.

Top Tasks to Outsource

What makes many online entrepreneurs tick, is the ability to wear many hats, simultaneously juggle dozens of duties, and multitask their way from start to finish to generate a revenue stream.

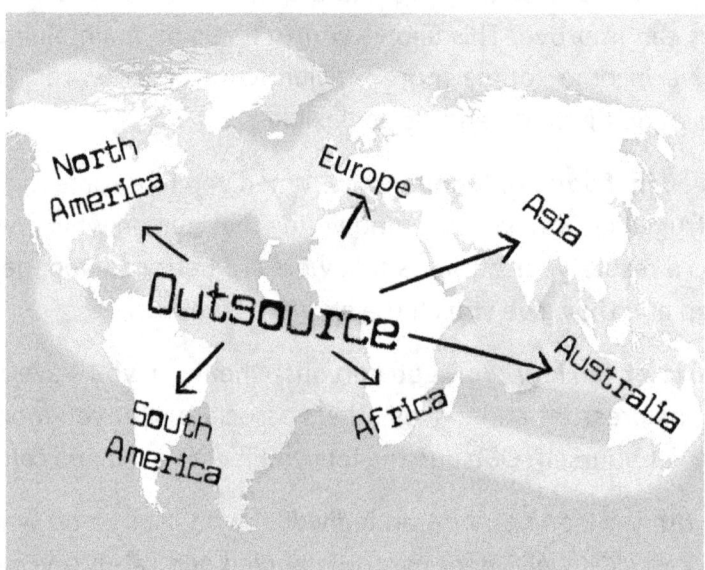

However, the consequences of intense multitasking can lower your productivity and may get as worse as affecting your brain negatively. Studies are rife with statistics and case studies illustrating the capabilities and limitations of the human brain to effectively perform more than one task at a time.

So what is the path to follow? One of the tactics is to slowly grow your business and allow yourself time to manage roles for which you are very good and that you are comfortable playing at any time.

Have you had enough of the current situation of your business? Do you want to increase your traffic, improve your conversions and boost your sales? The way forward is to outsource specific and tedious tasks so that you can save time as you grow your business and skyrocket your passive income using the right platform.

Conversion Optimization

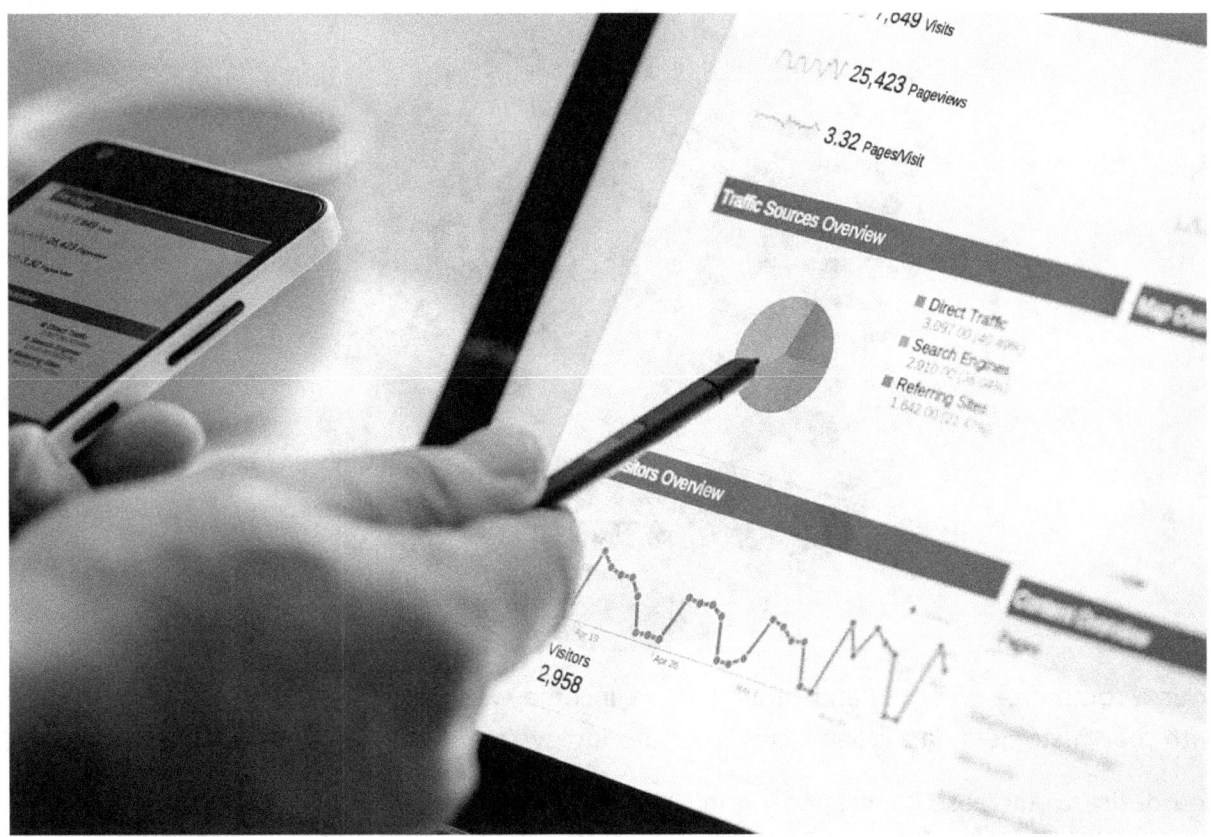

Approximately 96% of individuals visiting your website may not commit to purchase from you. This means either you need to optimize your conversions for higher sales and profit, or you're satisfied with living off the 4% of the customers you actually sell to. This should not be your lot! There are so many conversion optimization experts you can hire at a very affordable rate.

The good news is that through content advertising, product reviews, and enhancements to your sales funnel, it is feasible to give your conversions a drastic boost.

But, do you know which one is going to work best for your business, and how they all work together? Rather than spending time and money on guessing and experimenting, outsource by finding the right expert for the job. The earlier you adopt this, the quicker you are going to take advantage of them and scale your way to the top.

Customer Support

Your e-commerce websites and other passive income websites are dead if you can't engage with your customers via a reliable customer support system.

You desire to increase conversions, don't you? Never ignore the power of reliable customer support. It may take years for entrepreneurs to fine-tune their reaching out and generate a constant revenue stream. But losing a customer's allegiance due to bad customer service can take just a few minutes. Hire a qualified virtual assistant in your niche and on the products and services that you're offering. Search through your network for suggestions, or use LinkedIn groups to discover someone who matches your requirements.

Customer service professionals can help you focus on most of your customers' contact channels. Live Chat assistance, for instance, can assist you to solve problems when a customer goes to your site for a solution or enquire about a product. This can help you close a sale by answering questions about your products and services instantly for customers who come visiting.

Lead Generation

The whole essence of lead generation is to increase conversions and boost sales.

If lead generation resulting from an increase in traffic was a simple process that anybody could venture doing, there wouldn't be so much continuous reports on online entrepreneurs' failures based on it. Like conversion optimization, lead generation is as critical and has a direct impact on how far your company can be scaled-up. It's also extremely time-consuming and technical. You therefore need to hire an expert in the field.

SEO

SEO or Search Engine Optimization is one part of online business strategies aimed at increasing traffic. The task of dealing with very effective optimization cuts across many areas. Experts are knowledgeable in various aspects of SEO. They will help you boost traffic to your website through your content and even social media. They will also assist with adequate platform setup. You shouldn't be troubled by this aspect if you consider outsourcing. By allocating a small budget, you will certainly find many expert freelancers willing and available for such a task.

Don't try to do it all by yourself if you desire productive and efficient business.

Of course, you may be feeling you have the whole situation under control; but trust me, you may soon feel overwhelmed or bored and even withdraw when things get burdensome. You may end up spending a lot of time on low-level assignments, starting to feel overworked, and never seem to have an opportunity to pursue operations that really excite you.

The easiest way to get rid of things that overcrowd your life is by eliminating them, outsource appropriately!

You may, perhaps, be thinking that asking for professional help in your business is a sign of weakness; NO! It isn't! This is a false belief!

Here's the straightforward truth: We would rather not request help since we think it makes us look powerless.

In contrast, requesting for help is a mature thing, one that has been practiced by the world's best entrepreneurs both online and offline. Who doesn't need help?

Need some help, don't you? Skyrocket your passive income business by exploring the Author's recommendations here: www.andymutambya.com.

Secret 3: What Are Your Customers' Needs, Wants and Desires?

Today's websites are dead for many reasons. One among them is the fact that many online entrepreneurs don't know what their customers are looking for over the internet.

What do you have to offer? Is it what your customers actually want? Are you in the right niche? Your passion may be good to chase up but it may not actually be what people are searching for online. You can be selling bananas to people looking to buy oranges! You should research the market to know exactly what people are searching for online and tailor your business to be in line with that by choosing a profitable niche.

What are you selling? Is it:

A. *Health,*
B. *Wealth or*
C. *Relationship?*

Human beings do not need to think twice to spend for any of these three. They are the top evergreen niche categories. The demand for them will always be positive no matter what, but it is your duty to work out the right sub-category among those three for your specific niche.

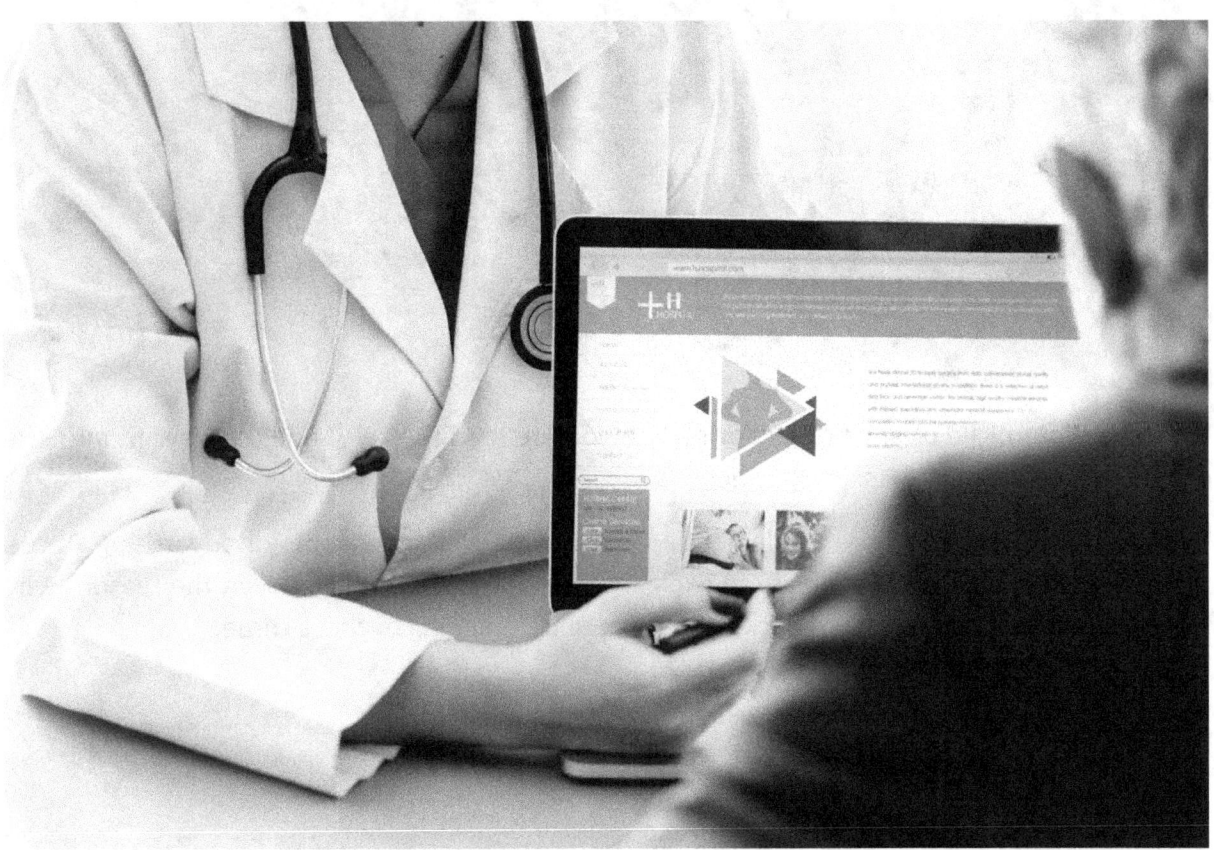

These are broad niche categories that already have a high concentration of businesses running them. To make an impact, you have to go niche-down, to the very specific. For instance, in the health niche, you can niche-down to supplements and further still to weight loss supplements. Have in mind that the niches you opt for may also have been populated by marketers. That shouldn't deter you though. All you need to do is to carve out a niche for yourself in the already saturated ecosystem. Approach things differently from the way others are doing. This way, you're going to sieve out your audience from the crowd and make a profit with your chosen business model.

Whatever your niche or any product or service you are trying to sell, should always fit into one of these three core markets. Be specific!

Needs, wants and desires are fundamental components of the concepts of advertising. These three words appear simple and easy to explain ideas on the surface. However, the reasons why websites are dead can be traced back to a lack of understanding of these three.

Let's look a little more deeply.

In terms of commercial management, wants, needs and desires play a crucial role. What is the key issues about these marketing concepts? Wants, Needs and desires assist us to create a powerful customer connection.

To put it in another way, understanding these concepts is vital to your sales increase and an overall success of your business. We, humans, have endless requirements and desires.

As marketing concepts, these three are linked but attend to different issues.

When there is a sense of impairment and our imagination needs something, we call it needs. Now, let's have a thorough debate of all three.

Needs: The simplest explanation of the notion of "needs" is the fundamental human needs such as shelter, clothing, and food. This definitely shows that which people will continually seek after to meet their needs.

If we take the subject further, needs can be extended down to other things such as training, services, healthcare, pension, etc.

If you intend to sell a product or service that falls under the category of "needs," you may have to work really hard.

This is because, in this day and age, thousands of brands are already providing services and products which meet the needs of people. You have to show something that distinguishes you from the rest to attract an audience.

Moreover, the demands are not just physical. Needs, for instance, can be a social thing that belongs to a certain community and needs to be attended to.

How do you help customers? How do you meet their needs?

- *Solve a problem*
- *Teach a technique*
- *Offer alternative methods*
- *Provide helpful information*
- *Give real value*

This is where online entrepreneurs come in. You must identify the needs of your customers and attend to them by offering solutions. To increase conversions and make more sales, problem-solving is a sure way to make the most impact. Show your customers the best way to do a thing. Answer the most questions bothering their minds. Teach them how to solve a problem and equip them with do-it-yourself skills and they'll keep coming after you knowing you care about them. This is one of the powerful sets of top secrets to help you skyrocket your passive income in no time.

Wants: This is a notion quite unlike requirements or needs. Wants can be likened to wishes.

Wishes aren't permanent, and they change frequently. As time goes by, individuals and place will alter accordingly. You must be very careful if you have to go with this category since things can change.

The Core Differences

Amongst the most basic ideas driving your marketing attempts is to understand the distinction between Wants and Needs. Some websites are dead because entrepreneurs don't know what they are into.

'Needs' represent the desire of a customer for an item, or service, or a particular gain. It could be as functional as food is to the body. Consider the basic necessities of life falling in this category.

Wants are desires that are not essential. It is typically recognized that once all basic needs have been fulfilled, the customer moves to want. Potable water, for instance, is a necessity, but carbonated water is a want.

What is essential as a marketer or as an online entrepreneur is to generate a desire in the mind of the customer, and to encourage them to take action, thereby converting their willingness to demand.

Solving customers' needs

If websites are dead today, one thing that may have led to that, could be traced back to entrepreneurs not being able to solve customers' problems efficiently.

A major component of growth and ability to increase traffic is at the disposal of every business owner when they're able to provide adequate solutions to their customers' needs.

Yes, customers can determine the sustainability and advancement of your online business but all lies in your hands to be there for them when they need a way out.

"You have to begin with the consumer skills and work back to the technology," noted Steve Jobs. "You can't start with the technology and try to figure out where you're going to sell it." Allow yourself to ignore this aspect and your websites will be dead before you know it!

How do you know the needs of your target audience? What needs to change in your business? Must other departments change their objectives?

If you have not been paying attention to your customers' problems before, navigating this field can be challenging and may even come with a hefty price tag.

So, to propel you in the right direction, here are tips for beginners, describing customers' needs. These guidelines will reveal the way you need to handle common barriers which prevent businesses from efficiently addressing clients' needs; they will unveil methods for continual improvement of customer support. Provide answers to these questions:

- What are the needs, wants and desires of your customers?
- What core category do they belong to?
- What is your assessment of your customers' requirements?
- What Customer Service type is preferable to better serve your clients?
- How do you solve your customers' needs?

A customer requirement illustrates the client's motivation to purchase a product or service. Ultimately, the need is the driver of the buying choice of the customer. Business owners often see a customer's need as an opportunity to go back to the drawing board and evaluate their original motive in order to meet the particular need.

Here are the most prevalent customer needs categories— many of which play nicely to move a buying decision. You should have knowledge about buyers' personas.

Customers want to buy based on some parameters:

1. Functionality- To fix their issue or desire, customers need your product or service to work the manner they desire.

#96115363

2. Price- Customers have a distinct budget to spend on a product or service.

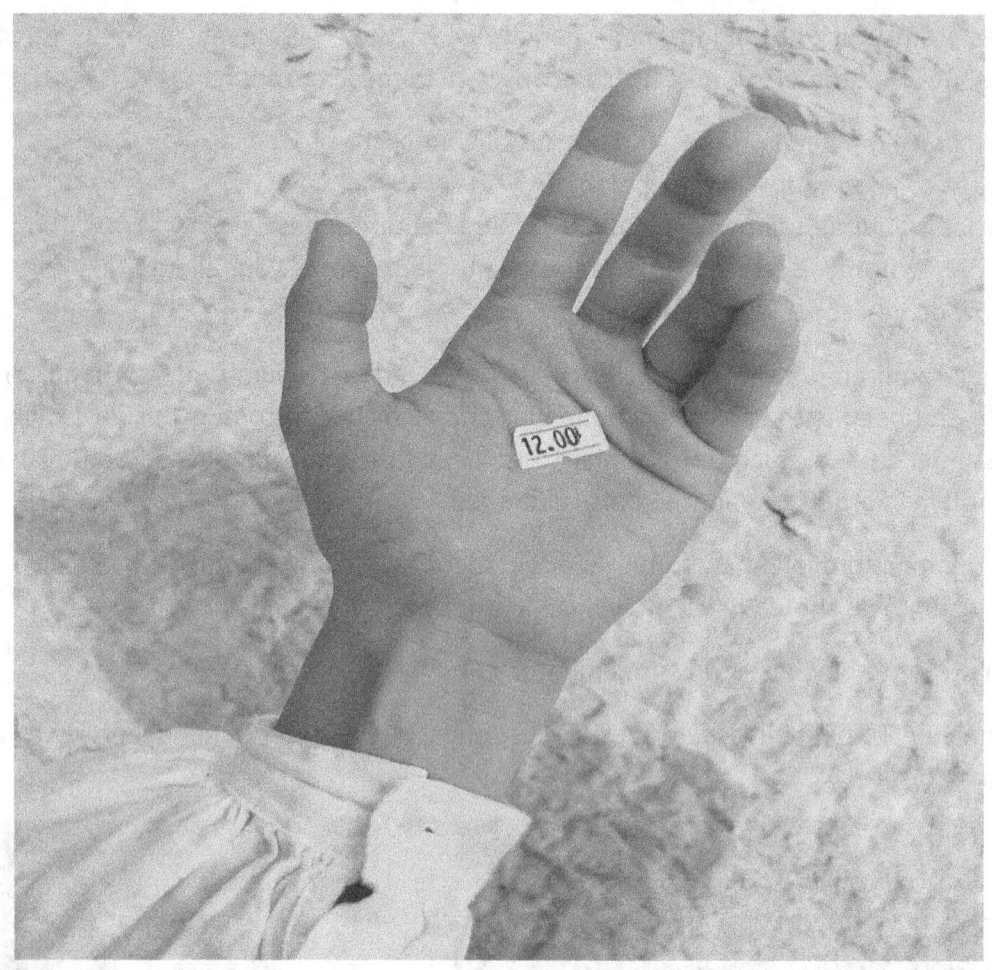

3. Convenience- How readily accessible and easy to use are your products and services to fulfill your customer's requirements.

4. Experience- The experience of a customer for using your product or service must be a positive or good one.

5. Design- To create it comparatively simple and intuitive to use, the product or service requires a slick design along the lines of experience.

6. Reliability- Each time the consumer wants to use it, the product or service must function reliably as advertised.

7. Performance- The goods or services must properly perform for the customer to achieve their objectives.

8. Efficiency- By streamlining what would otherwise be a time-consuming process, the product or service must be efficient.

9. Compatibility- Your product must be consistent with other products already in use by your customer and in-line with their requirements.

10. Empathy- When your customers come into contact with your customer service, your staff ought to be compassionate and understanding while helping them.

11. Fairness- From sales and service terms, up to after sales terms and throughout the duration of any agreement, customers expect a business to be fair.

12. Transparency- Customers demand full transparency from any business they deal with. From service breakdowns, price shifts, and any other related event, customers deserve openness from businesses they are giving their cash to.

13. Control- Customers ought to feel that they are in control of interaction with your business from beginning to end and beyond. Customer empowerment should not end with the purchase. Make returning products easy for them; flexibility in changing subscriptions, in adjusting terms, etc.

14. Options- When customers get prepared to buy from a business, they need alternatives. To provide that liberty of choice, offer a range of products, subscriptions and payment possibilities.

15. Information- Customers ought to be informed from the moment they come in contact with your business up to days and weeks after they make a purchase. Businesses need to invest in informative blog contents, educational contents and periodic communication via email series and other modes to provide customers with needed info for successful use of products and services.

16. Accessibility- Customers must have access to your service teams and support staff. This implies offering various customer service channels.

Customers are attracted based on meeting their underlying needs and sustained through the enforcement of business values.

What is the assessment of customers' requirements?

In product design and branding, a customer requirement assessment is used to provide an in-depth assessment to guarantee that the product or service delivers the characteristics necessary to give value to the customer.

To effectively carry out a customer requirement assessment, you must do the following:

1. Customer Needs Analysis Survey: Customer requirement analysis is typically performed by conducting surveys that assist businesses in figuring out how they stack up to meet the needs of their target customers in their various competitive industries.

The study should primarily ask questions about your brand and that of your competitors or rivals, as well as about the customers' knowledge of the product and the overall performance of the brand in the market.

Questions may include:

- Questions requesting customers to relate your brand with competing products
- Questions about comparing and filtering products based on their usage preferences

2. **Means-End Analysis:** Once the customer needs assessment study has been performed, you can use the responses to get a more complete image of why your customers buy from you and what distinguishes your particular product from your rivals.

Means-end assessment analyses these responses to evaluate the main reasons for buying your item by your customers. These buyers' reasons can be divided into three primary groups:

• Features: Due to the attributes included in the descriptions, a customer may be motivated to purchase a given service or product. For instance, a customer may purchase a smartphone from you because it is lighter than other alternatives.

• Benefits: Because of a given benefit, customers may agree to purchase a service or product that they believe will meet their needs. As an example, a customer may buy a particular smartphone because of its readiness to synchronize wirelessly with their appliances.

• Values: Customers purchase products or services for distinctive values, which they're convinced will help them satisfy some of their needs. Customers may be persuaded that by owing a particular smartphone, it will help them become more innovative or creative and discover other private or professional possibilities.

The reasons for buying a specified item can differ from one customer to another, as you're aware! So, it is essential to perform these customer surveys, gather the responses, and sort them into those three classifications. This study will allow you to work out which of the variables you should focus on in order to solve your customers' problems and be able to enhance or create your service or product to be more competitive on the market.

3. **Customer Service Types**: In consideration of online entrepreneurs' ability to efficiently solve problems, the communication system utilized to react to customers' demands plays a significant role. Some customers' requirements are sensitive and involve instant mobile or chat communication. Let's break down customer service tools and examine how each maximizes the capacity of your team to meet customer requirements.

Some of the tools to use to help solve your customers' needs

Email:

Email communication is among customer service's most basic tools. It enables customers to adequately explain their issues and allows easy exchange of documents. Customers should need to explain their problems only once, while customer care representatives can refer to significant details of the case without requesting extra data.

Email is better used for customer requirements that need not be addressed immediately. Once the customer service representative has resolved the problem, customers will still be able to review their initial query, go back to the issue and revisit the solution.

Unfortunately, the inability of customers to clearly explain their issues is one downside of email communication. Some customers may have difficulty to describe their issues through email communication, and some service reps may also experience some limitations in explaining solutions. This can be time-consuming when the problem is too complex. Email use should be limited to fairly easier and simpler issues requiring a short explanation or solution.

Telephone:

This is an appropriate channel to use when customers have issues that need to be addressed instantly. Telephones directly connect customers with the business and generate a human relationship between the customer and the business. This human factor is an important feature in ensuring good customer experience.

Phone calls can come in even more useful when dealing with a frustrated or upset customer. Such customers will mostly require a personalized solution from your team. Both sides hear the voice, the tone of each other and the intensity of the scenario can be measured and have an impact on the outcome. Soft communication skills should be used by your team to appease the customer. The answers provided do sound more authentic over phones.

Waiting time is the most prevalent defect with phone assistance. Customers dislike being placed on hold. Studies suggest that if a call is dropped while on hold, more than a quarter of your customers will not return to do business with you. Therefore, your phone connection should be designated for issues requiring instant, hands-on assistance.

Chat:

Chat system is the most versatile customer care service. It can solve a large number of easy issues or provide complicated ones with adequate assistance. Businesses continue to embrace chat for its versatility and improved efficiency for customer service. Chat could be used to address almost any problem when it comes to customer needs. Chatbots can answer simple and popular questions because of its automated customer service. Online entrepreneurs can incorporate such customer service instruments into their conversation apps to help them identify and timely solve problems however easy or sophisticated they may appear.

Chat limitations are similar to email limitations. However, any absence of clarity between the two sides can have a drastic effect on troubleshooting as chat communication is live.

Social Networks:

This is a fairly new channel for customer service. It is progressively being adopted by a large number of companies as a feasible service alternative. That's because social networking allows customers to report problems instantly. The fact that problems are mostly posted in public, customer service teams are bound to respond in a manner that upholds the business image.

Social networking is an outstanding channel for global communication, it is an efficient tool for large-scale communication with your customers. During crisis moments, your team can use this channel to maintain contact with your customers and continue to meet their needs.

Mass media is distinct from other customer service communication channels because it gives the most power to the customer. Folks tend to have more pressing issues and expect you to respond instantly. While this sort of service offers a tremendous privilege, it also puts tremendous pressure on you to meet customers demand. Make sure that your team has adequate social media marketing instruments in place.

There is no such a thing as the best customer service channel! Each tool complements the other when used together to increase sales. This provides your customers with a great communication experience that will make them come back for more business.

Now that you are acquainted with these important forms of customer service, let's explore what needs to be done by your team to meet specific customer requirements.

How to Solve Customers' Needs?

The first step to solving your customers' problems is to put yourself in their shoes:

If you were the customer in the process of buying your goods, using your technology, or signing up for your services or facilities, what would deter you from achieving the ultimate goal?

1. **Offer Coherent Messaging Throughout**

Too often customers get caught up in a game of being told that a product can do one thing, only to discover later on that this is not the case. Ultimately, customers are confused and leave.

One of the finest steps towards a more consumer-focused mindset is consistent internal messaging across all channels. If the entire organization understands its objectives, values, product and service strengths, thus the messages can easily be translated to meet the needs of customers.

2. **Provide Easy-to-use Instructions**

Customers buy a product because they trust that their needs will be met and their problems solved. Your descriptions and directions ought to be clear and succinct. If from the very beginning, best practices aren't specified and your customers don't see value straight away, it's almost an exercise in futility to try and regain their confidence.

One way businesses obtain and maintain their customers attention is to provide in-product guidelines as quickly as a payment approval is received by the customer, if not before. This lowers confusion, and technical issues.

A customer education manual or knowledge-base is crucial for adequate customer implementation. It is especially useful whenever customers find themselves stuck.

3. **Request Feedback From Customers**

Pay close attention and learn from complaints and suggestions from your customers and it will change your way of doing business and allow you to better serve them.

Treat customer suggestions seriously and act on them to enhance design, product and possible system failures. Most metrics of customer support are essential to the user experience and this mindset should go down to every component of your organization.

Businesses gain and maintain track of feedbacks via customer satisfaction results, customer surveys, customer interviews, social media surveys. They also capture helpful customer feedback via private emails.

4. **Nurture Connections with Customers**

When a customer purchases a product or service, they immediately want to use it and meet their instant needs. Whether they're delighted in the first hour, week or month, it's important to think about their current needs constantly.

Proactive connections are essential to prevent customers from losing their enthusiasm after a purchase. If consumers stop hearing from you and vice versa, this may indicate that their business continuity with you is threatened.

Online entrepreneurs and marketers are expected to be able to solve a mixture of customer service issues, establish communication strategies and a support team for customer interactions and retention.

5. Solve Customers' Requirements

Addressing the needs of your customers and clearly defining the wishes you can meet and the ones you cannot, is a significant step towards solving urgent problems. It is not possible to treat all customer requirements equally, and businesses have to acknowledge which issues they can fix and those that do not fit their vision.

From start-ups, various marketers, online entrepreneurs and all the way up to the likes of Fortune 500 companies, all meaningfully address and prioritize customer requirements in such a way that keeps them ahead of the competition while achieving success.

How does your business solve the requirements and needs of your customers? For helpful insights, take a look at the Author`s recommendations at www.andymutambya.com.

Secret 4: Why and How Must You Hack Your Influencer?

Hardly can a passive income business or marketing entrepreneur do well today without effectively using appropriate influencers' marketing strategies.

Modelling influencers' tactics is the coolest and most powerful marketing trend right now! This technique is one of the top 7 weird secrets to increase your traffic, conversions, and sales. Social media has acquired such a big influence on the digital marketing world that virtually anyone can become an influencer in a particular industry and it is your duty to pick the right ones.

Who is an online influencer?

An online influencer is simply an individual on the internet who has a strong influence on others. He or she dictates what other people do by leading the way. If they buy a product, their followers will do the same, trusting their judgment. When influencers talk, their supporters listen and are motivated to take action accordingly. Online entrepreneurs take advantage of this system to increase sales.

Celebrities tend to come to mind when talking about influencers but it doesn't have to be, this concept goes far beyond that. In fact, the majority of non-celebrity influencers do better in this game than the so-called celebrities. By modelling them appropriately, influencers will help lift your business.

But who are those influencers? Are they all our favorite and famous singers, performers, and celebrities? Well, not necessarily! While these individuals are certainly influencers, this is not the criteria to be one.

Online influencers referred to here, are those guys vlogging on their YouTube channels or posting cool photos on Instagram; they are the so-called YouTubers, Instagrammers, etc. The number of their followers may range from thousands to millions of people and their rates of engagement is mostly much higher than many celebrities'. They are not a substitute for celebrities, but in today's online business set up, they are certainly in control when it comes to an effective marketing of products and services. It is not difficult to understand why most websites are dead today! Many online entrepreneurs and marketers are yet to grasp the techniques of modelling influencers for their passive income businesses.

Influencers can be:

- Speakers
- Bloggers
- Digital marketers
- Product creators
- Designers
- Affiliate marketers
- Information marketers
- Creators of Facebook pages
- Product promoters and so on

For every business type or niche, there is an influencer. Smart online entrepreneurs make finding, studying and modelling their preferred influencers, an important part in their business set up.

There is no hard and fast rule about who an influencer can be. Every influencer can be identified based on what they do and what you're after. You can't just pick anybody based merely on their level of popularity, No! That particular individual must have influence over a particular industry or niche.

Working with an influencer has been proven to be much more cost-effective, efficient and fruitful than using services of huge media organizations. This is largely because influencers have their own groups of faithful supporters following them and who are ready to commit and willing to make a purchasing choice.

Are your websites dead? Now that you know the advantages of influencer marketing, how do you make the most of it? There are a few things you can do.

Search out appropriate influencers. Particularly, if your product is not a mainstream one, it may not be a straightforward process to locate the right micro-influencers fitting your needs. It would be a waste of time and money to use non-relevant influencers. So, make sure you invest sufficient time to find the right one for your business, products or offers.

But the key point here is to allow the influencer to convey the message using their voice and style. It may not be a good idea to give them exactly what they should be saying. Just offer them the item and allow them to experiment. They are better positioned to know what their followers will like or dislike.

Let the influencer tell your target audience a selling story. The conventional practice of just holding your product in their hands is old school now; one post in the background with your product won't work! So, make sure you have a proper plan to let your influencer tell your story. Nowadays, people relate to stories that are able to take them through an imaginary journey in order to justify their purchases.

Why must you Hack your Influencer?

There are a few reasons why a business might want to use a marketing influencer:

- They drive real engagement
- The voice of an influencer is authentic
- An influencer can help create social buzz
- They are much more cost-effective than celebrities
- An influencer can use local / community marketing wisely?
- They can be very specific and brand-relevant

So how do you get to present your product or service to those big influencers?

Authenticity is a major factor in influencer marketing. Be real and authentic with what you do. You should stand out and be known to do things in a unique way. Influencers will be more attracted to work with you when they know you have a distinct product.

It's like asking for a referral or a recommendation from a friend because you're certain they want the best for you. So, if you had to define it, influencer marketing takes the voice of an influencer to give approval to your product or service and engender genuine commitment from influencer followers.

Hacking your Influencer

You need to identify who is the best or successful business person in your particular market and model them. This is exactly what it takes for most ordinary marketers and entrepreneurs to suddenly turn into the greatest online money-making machines! This is the real hack you should adopt for your business model because it works with every niche and business type.

How do you hack your influencer to attract your dream buyers?

Hack your influencer's ad, hook, story and offer to attract your dream customers. These are all different types of content. Great content helps online entrepreneurs and marketers retain their customers and invite prospects; they are informative and interesting, never boring in any way!

Let's explore these influencer hacking techniques in detail

Hook

The hook could be an image, headline, video or something else used to grab someone's attention. Influencers are good with this tool. What engaging content do you have to capture your audience attention? You should do this constantly. How do influencers and other smart entrepreneurs implement all these in their businesses? Study them carefully and adopt the same for your business. You should ultimately model your influencer's hook while being ethical.

Story

If your websites are dead and not attracting attention or enough traffic, not achieving targeted conversions and sales, you must develop your storytelling skills.

Now that you have caught someone's attention with an appealing hook, you need to tell them a story. Likeable stories stick more in the brain and help businesses find success. How do your influencers tell their stories? Model yours after theirs. You stand a better chance to tell your own stories about yourself and business. You can use social media platforms such as Facebook, Instagram, YouTube and so on for your storytelling. Stories are easy to understand. People connect with stories much faster and remember them much more easily.

Offer

Sell an offer, not a product. You sell your product cheaper to your customers by adding value, not by lowering the price! An offer is about combining your products in such a way that their value is increased by presenting them bundled together.

Your offer has to fulfill on the promise that your sales message made. This is why online entrepreneurs give protection to their buyers by providing them with a guarantee that the product works as described. And if it doesn't, a refund can be requested. This concept justifies why you should always start with a sales message and not the offer.

Setting Yourself Apart from the Competition

The way you make and present your offer by raising your products' potential value will set you apart from competitors. This is the catalyst for your success!

In contrast to what we've learned in college, you should always go after the Red Ocean. This simply represents the hot market, the hot traffic! We have been taught to shy away from the big crowds, the big markets; this is why many entrepreneurs and their websites are failing!

As an entrepreneur, to become a money-making machine, you have to be bold and hang out in areas where people spend a lot of money. You must then hack wisely and ethically the techniques of your influencers to attract the customers of your dreams.

Lack of traffic is one of the major reasons why many websites are dead.

Online entrepreneurs should know that consumers' problems are specific to each customer. Study and identify each consumer as per the nature of the traffic that visits your website. Traffic is one sure way to revive your business. Therefore knowing and attracting the right traffic is crucial for your business survival.

Traffic Types

Hot Traffic: These are consumers who are conscious of their needs and aware of the likely solutions, but perhaps not quite knowledgeable of your kind of solution.

Warm Traffic: They are customers who know their problems but do not know how to solve them.

Cold Traffic: They are consumers who have no idea about their problems or solutions.

Those are the different types of traffic that online entrepreneurs face in their everyday businesses.

The SECRET is to just focus on HOT TRAFFIC, since that's where your DREAM CUSTOMERS are hanging out.

Hot traffic because your ideal clients are already aware of their problems and the kind of solutions they are expecting to help solve those problems. It is now for you to proffer solutions to help solve those issues. Tailor your business after your customers' needs; as a result, increased conversions and sales will come following.

We were taught to avoid competition, wrong! You need to unlearn that and focus on selling an offer, not a product! Add real value and stand out from competition!

Hacking Strategies:

Identify your influencer from the red ocean and model them by following ethical and moral values. Copy their style and implement their strategies.

You need to find out if and how much your influencers are spending on publishing and what is keeping them in a particular business.

The blue ocean represents the approach derived from the influencer's tactics. After modeling your influencer from the red ocean, you then create your blue ocean with the way you present your own product or service. Use your influencer's marketing pattern, add value and sell to the same customers.

You sell in the red ocean without engaging in any competition within that pool.

Your hacking strategies should cover the following:

Marketing

Marketing can be described as the act of changing someone's belief with the intention of leading them to make a purchase. Marketing cuts across many channels as you'll see in other sections of this book.

Selling

This is the act of presenting an offer while overcoming objections. You must stop trying to convince people to buy from you – Why?

It's all about adding value! Online entrepreneurs create and retain new customers by adding value. If all your customers can see, is that you are only interested in making money on their backs, do not be surprised to see them leave one after the other.

Consumers are more and more reluctant to buy from strangers. Build a good rapport with your prospects first. You need to take them on a journey or an experience leading them to want to do business with you. This is the way sales funnels work! They represent a sales process from point A to Z; from drawing the customer's attention to the point of making a sale and beyond.

Closing

Closing a sale relates to logical reasoning leading customers to act now. It may be channeled through a message of urgency or scarcity which makes customers pay you instantly in exchange for your offer.

What are the most powerful marketing steps and strategies?

a. Ads

Paid ads are very important parts of today's marketing. They exist in various forms. Social media ads like Facebook ads and Google AdWords make up some of the most powerful ad methods used by marketers and online entrepreneurs to increase traffic, improve conversions and boost sales.

Direct Response Marketing

We are fortunate to be living in this age of direct response marketing possibilities; which means that we have the capacity to be able to directly assess the performance of each ad we put out there. This helps us evaluate, almost instantly, whether an ad is making us any money or not. This is where popular tools such as analytics and other data evaluation tools come in.

Warning: One of the most powerful sets of secrets to help you become a money-making machine as an online entrepreneur or marketer is not to immediately withdraw your earnings from your first advertising campaign. You have to roll your earnings back in around 8 to 10 times or until you reach a point of ad-fatigue. At this point, your ad no longer follows the same conversion pattern as in the previous steps, this is when you can start taking your earnings out.

b. Landing Page

The main purpose of creating an attractive, yet informative landing page is to capture your audience's contact information, such as name, email address, phone number, physical address, and more. This is usually a single page. Landing pages should be well-designed. They drive visitors to take action. The layout of a landing page is distinct, succinct and straight to the point. Typically, landing pages incorporate a bait in the form of a freebie used to persuade potential customers to give away their email addresses or other contact info in exchange for the giveaway. Your offer can be an eBook, software or something valuable that they will appreciate and for which you will not incur expensive fulfillment or inventory costs.

The LIST:

Building a list is the cornerstone of every business. The main purpose of a landing page is to help you build a list of customers to whom you can market your product continuously.

In this day of technological progress, almost every smartphone owner checks his email or SMS more than once a day; as an online entrepreneur or marketer, you cannot afford to ignore such a readily available pool of potential customers.

After gathering your customers' contact info, your landing page guides them towards the next steps of the journey or sales funnel, with the intention of selling them your precious offers; hence allowing you the possibility to quickly recoup your ad money and break even much sooner.

Once they're on your list, this means that almost everything you sell to them afterwards becomes juicy and free income for you as you're no longer paying for any costly ad in order to sell to them, since you've already got them on your precious clients' list!

c. Sales Page

If you hardly have any sale, your websites are dead! The next step in the sales funnel from the landing page is the sales page. The sales page allows you to present your offer to your prospects. It is normally a one-page design as well. Sell your products by highlighting their benefits instead of their features. Users are more interested in values your products will add to them than mere features they contain.

d. One Time Offer (OTO) page for your upsells

Besides the front-end products, upsells are a great way for online entrepreneurs to generate more income. Customers are motivated to buy your upsells when such has the potential to add additional value to them.

You need a hook, story, and offer structures at each of those stages of marketing.

By getting your message or copy right, combining it with the right platform and audience, you won't need to try and convince anyone to buy from you. The right buyers will be attracted without any more effort from you.

You have to model the best there is to accomplish the best method for your business.

The best way to make use of influencer marketing is by hacking them in order to drive reliable marketing business for yourself.

Hack your influencers' contents, their formats and apply them to your online business while staying within ethical and moral norms throughout the whole process.

How to Create an Influencer Marketing Strategy?

As a recap, the strategy to effectively drive influencer marketing for online business entails the following steps:

1. Finding appropriate influencers for your product, service, offer or business
2. Reaching out and connecting with them
3. Spreading your ideas and sales messages through your selected influencers
4. Monitoring the effectiveness of your selected influencer's marketing strategy

It is a misleading myth to think that Influencers are only people who have lots of followers and likes on platforms such as Twitter, LinkedIn, Instagram, YouTube, Facebook pages and so on. The type of influencer you may need, may be an ordinary individual with just enough online presence and with the capacity to lead their fans to take a buying decision.

Why?

Why search for your true and appropriate influencer? Because hosting a good profile picture, then buying a lot of followers is extremely easy! Don't be misled!

Truth is, for genuine influencers, the important thing is not to have hundreds of thousands of followers. What matters most is to have a good amount of interactions with their fans.

Now, to discover true influencers, you need to make sure you spend your time and energy with the right crowds.

How to Search and Discover the Right Influencer?

Relevance is the number one challenge; but there are others too. For instance, many scammers purchase fake follows and likes, then pose as influencers with the intention of ripping off unsuspecting customers. You must therefore make diligent investigations. Be sure to check the influencer's public account or social media channels to avoid such unpleasant outcomes. You may also hire someone to carry out required inquiries on your behalf in case you do not have sufficient time or knowledge, by using the "who" strategy as referred to earlier on in this book.

This is broken down into a sequence of measures

- Searching the web
- Using appropriate tools
- Making a list

The first thing is to do a search online, then using search engines and tools as appropriate, make a list of top social media influencers in your business category. In one way, this helps to narrow down who you want to speak to according to your niche. You can then do more advanced and targeted searches based on your business intentions.

Breaking down the search:

For instance:

Content marketing- you intend to discover influencers on content marketing.

Influencers- because that's what you're looking for.

Twitter- This is a platform you may be active on and the people you want to connect with are also available on that platform according to the search results. Therefore, connecting with them is incredibly simple that way.

Now that you've worked out your niche, it's time to discover the right influencers, the correct way.

Tools:

Using Tools such as Statusbrew may be a good choice if you know about the software and how it works.

Statusbrew helps to segment customers in their profile according to keywords and sort them out based on their supporters. Then, the most important feature, is the function of the filter "Tweets per Day", supplied with the tool, allowing you to filter out the less active profiles. Constant activity is more than important for an influencer.

Then the next in line of tools should be Buzzsumo. Its domain authority feature is the target here. Using Buzzsumo authority metric can help you make an informed decision about who you should be talking to.

It also shows the content recently shared by influencers. This helps in guiding you through the type of content that will interest your prospective influencers.

There are other helpful tools you can also explore such as Klear and Kred.

Klear allows you to filter out individuals according to various criteria such as social networks, influence, skills, location and even the average age of the audience.

Kred, in addition to other data such as Influence score, Kred gives a helpful outreach score because it tells how probable your content could be shared. This is similar to the Statusbrew's 'Tweets per day' filter.

Making a List of Influencers

List making should be the last step to take using this strategy. At this stage, you ought to compare all the influencers discovered using the various tools, then compile a list of all of them.

Now, this is not just another list! This is a list compiled based on your ability to interact with selected influencers, taking into account important factors such as the social network they use prominently, their interests, the type of content they share, their influence score, their expertise…

This makes the process of finding and connecting with new influencers very simple and timely achievable.

How do you connect to influencers in your niche?

Read Their Stuff

Here's the first influencer marketing advice: Get to know about the influencer! Do not approach an influencer without at least reading some of their content. Make sure you've read or watched, at least, one of their articles or publication! One of the most powerful ways, is to sign up and respond to your influencers' newsletters. This makes you an active participant in their online community. If you want to work with them on some content marketing, you will definitely need to read, at least, a few of their blog posts. For their brand, their story and their audience, you really need to get a feeling!

Pitching Influencers

Make your email brief when you connect with them. Some influencers receive hundreds of emails each week from individuals or brands wishing to partner with them. Hence, a content-loaded outreach email often gets simply deleted. You'll want to use a creative subject line; in this case, keep your email short, and provide them with the necessary links to your brand.

Pitches that get the best response rates appear to have sufficient info equilibrium but leave the influencers curious about details. You can use a drip throughout the campaign to give your influencers some information and keep them engaged without overwhelming them!

It may be useful to know their charges at the beginning. This will allow you to negotiate and determine if they fit the scope or your project budget before you start talking about the campaign. Do not hesitate to ask them for this information if necessary.

As opposed to traditional PR, one of the main differences, when pitching influencers, is that they are mostly paid per post. Marketing influencers are so highly in demand nowadays that they tend to have more pitches than many conventional PR.

That's why your emails should be engaging and able to make influencers understand that the niche of your brand aligns with their publications. Note that influencers are paid per post. It is therefore crucial to highlight what your brand is willing to pay for their post. Once your influencer has responded to your initial pitch, take the time to share the campaign information while discussing about their pricing.

Once engaged, influencers will be more open to learning about your brand and campaign. Fortunately, if you're just starting out with influencer marketing, there are a lot of posts and case studies online to get you up to speed.

Find out what other brands that align with yours have accomplished in the past. Look at the tactics that brought them juicy ROI and apply them to your brand. Influencers tend to specialize in niches, rather than following just vertical patterns. It is also essential to know your customers before searching for appropriate influencers. This powerful influencer identification process allows marketers and online entrepreneurs to identify influencers for their brand. Even if you're an expert, it's also beneficial for you to understand how like-minded brands work with influencers.

Should you reach out to your competitors in your search for influencers in your niche?

The simple reply is "yes!"

Reaching out to or researching a competitor's blogs can help you partner with influencers in a similar niche. Through this process, you may also develop creative ideas on how to work with them.

This helps to confirm that the influencer has an affinity with the brand, product or service.

Get to Know Their Personal Info

Try to find out about your influencers ' personal data. Knowing their birthday, the size of their clothes or their favorite holiday destination will enable your brand to participate at a private level with them. This makes them feel unique for being part of your brand. Influencer pitching works best when it is an ongoing strategy as opposed to a one-time contact.

Using a customer relationship management (CRM) software or a spreadsheet software, you can save personal information about your influencers, enabling you to send them a surprise package containing the best products from your brand or just to wish them a happy anniversary. It may seem like a small thing, but it does contribute a lot in creating and sustaining an existing relationship.

Use the "Contact" page

Using the contact page of influencers can help you boost your relationship with them.

Be sure to keep your message short and provide links to your brand so that all the necessary information is available to the influencer.

It doesn't take a lot of time and it's worth trying.

How to Find the Email of an Influencer

There are numerous tools out there that can help you find any personal email address. Most come with a fee, but some of them have free options. Using LinkedIn may be your first step. Make a search about a company's executive director on LinkedIn by looking up their first and last name, you can then find their email address and connect with them.

But what do you do if the email is not posted on LinkedIn by that individual? Or what if your invitation is not answered? You can still find it out in seconds using one of these valuable platforms:

- AnyMailFinder
- Email Hunter

Using Your Paid Influencer Marketing Brand Content

Try changing tactics in case you realize consumers are not listening to your brand.

By changing the info you put on social network and using content that your influencers create for your brand, may help you readjust your tactics. Ask them first if your paid social campaigns will allow the use of their content. Don't copy and paste on your platform, make adjustments and edit as required before publishing.

Equipping yourself with Right Influencer Marketing Support (tools)

Without the help of an influencer marketing tool, it is almost impossible to implement influencer marketing effectively. There are many equally effective tools online for launching influencer marketing. A lot of these tools offer free trial packages, allowing you to carry out a test drive in order to work out which one works best for your brand. Determine which features meet your goals before making your final choice. Tools such as GroupHigh have powerful identification features for influencers. Doing a simple search on Google will also help you uncover the right tools for your goals.

Pitching influencers allows you to get them to work for your brand. This allows you to tap in one of the most effective marketing hacking techniques indeed!

For more on influencers, find help and author's recommendations at ww.andymutambya.com.

Secret 5: Why and How Must You Be Noisy and Create Mass Movement?

You've got to consistently publish your content. One of the main reasons why websites are dead is because passive income business owners are not utilizing every tool within their reach to get the messages about their products or services out there to people who actually need them. It's your job to spark the excitement of your products for your potential customers.

Making the most noise does not come from any content. It must be high quality content that your followers or potential customers will like. Teach an idea, help them solve a problem and add value to their lives through the publication of consistent content.

Take advantage of the different content formats and have a habit of making noise for the growth of your business. If you like to read, you can think of yourself as a blogger, if you prefer watching videos, you can also make your content available to other video consumers or maybe you like listening to podcasts, you should start podcasting as well so that others can learn from you.

Important facts for entrepreneurial success:

Make Noise with Ads

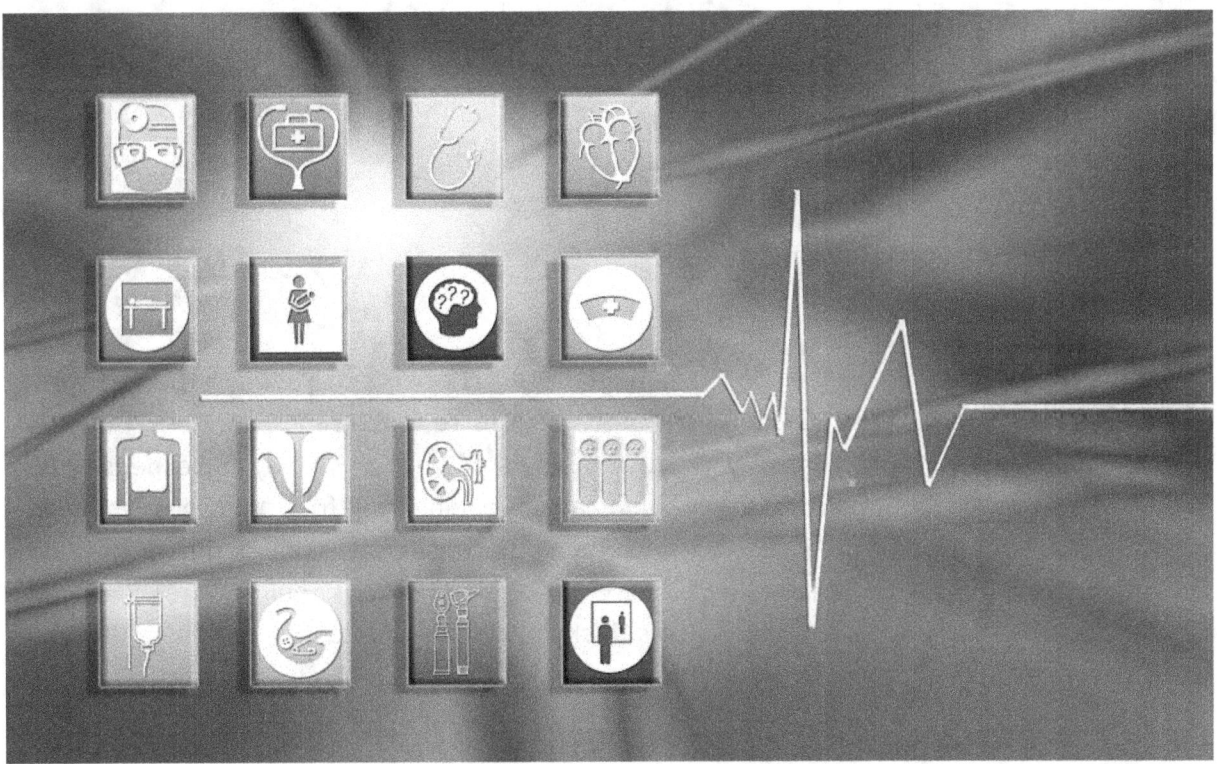

Entrepreneurs who spend more on ads, makes more money. Some websites are dead because some entrepreneurs do not see the real value of ad campaigns.

Ad campaigns are veritable tools in the hands of marketers who know how to effectively exploit their potential. You can grow your business much faster if you smartly make use of paid ads for your campaigns. By using ads, you get the most out of your business much faster. Google AdWords and social media networks such as Facebook are very good advertisement vehicles or platforms that you can leverage for your passive income success.

Publish where your audience hangs out

In case you're not prepared to spend on ads, you can rest assured that many publishing platforms also allow you to control your audience without having to pay for expensive ads. Everything is not all about paid ads before you can start benefiting from your passive income business. But you must be prepared to invest your other resources such as time and energy, because there is no such a thing as free. Every publication you post online takes you a step further towards reaching your business goals of skyrocketing your passive income and turning you into that online money-making machine.

The type of content you place on your website determines the relationship between your audience and your business. Identify your clients' needs and deliver high quality content to meet each of their demands, depending on the type of business you run. Keep in mind that you get the most attention from your audience when you prioritize their needs and offer solutions to meet them.

Make your audience come after you and not you going after them

You get to have hungry buyers hunting you, not you chasing after them; you start becoming your customers' prey! What more could you ask for in your network marketing or passive income business? If you do things right by publishing solutions that help your customers and providing products and services that add them value, it won't be long before increased traffic, conversion and sales start chasing you.

Your customers will start doing your bidding. They will promote your products to their friends, family and loved ones. It becomes like a springboard where turns of events start working in your favor. But initially, you have to pay the price by adding value to your audience in order to gain their trust and loyalty. Even your customers will start working for you by referring you to their loved ones without you asking them. Online entrepreneurs who have paid the price at the development stage of their businesses can afford to sit back later on and enjoy what they've sown in the past through hard work and by doing things right in the early phases of their businesses.

Choosing a Platform

What platform best fits your niche? Choosing a good platform that helps your publishing should be desired.

One of the most effective publishing hacks is to use a single platform before thinking about repurposing your content by republishing it differently online. As you start, trying to be everywhere on all platforms is not the best idea! Stick with one platform first to publish your content. For instance, if you market your product via a social media platform such as Facebook, be sure to develop it first before moving on to others. If you publish simultaneously on all existing social media platforms, you may end up overwhelmed with a dispersed audience and you may not have enough time to attend to each one of your potential customers.

When you stick with a platform at the initial stage, your audience will be aware of where to go when they need your assistance. Only move to other platforms when you've established your first platform properly. Keep in mind that you're not going to copy and paste the content from your established platform into every other one you're moving on to. Each platform has its unique way of publishing content to yield the best results. It is not how you publish content on Facebook that you're going to publish the same on Instagram or Twitter. You must repurpose each content in such a way that it meets the requirements of every platform.

Redistribute your content

Once your brand reputation is established on one platform, you can spread your content on many others just in case some of them fail. Don't just pick the systems that you like, let the market demand be your compass, follow it all through.

You need to properly pick which platform to use for publishing your content. Internet is the only place where you can publish and be able to be you.

What do you need to create mass movement?

Many online entrepreneurs are yet to discover the reasons why some businesses attract mass movement over the internet than others. What justifies this?

Three things you need:

Cause

If you have no cause in your online business, you may as well consider your websites as dead!

Many business websites are dead because, very often, online entrepreneurs lose grip of the reasons for creating those sites in the first place. Your cause will drive your passive income business to success. If nothing is urging you to start a passive income business, then you don't have any business going ahead with such a project.

The creation of a mass movement around your business should be considered as one of the future-based causes. It is a cause that seems very important for all charismatic leaders. Take a look at great leaders who are attracting mass movements. All of them have one thing in common, a futuristic cause they are pursuing.

History has proven how great religious and political leaders have also carried out mass movements around the globe by pursuing a specific cause. You must have a picture of what you're after to get.

Attractive Character

It takes an attractive character or charismatic leader to drive a cause. You cannot get it right with having mass movement around your business without presenting yourself as someone to be listened to. Your personality must show an attractive character. What do you have inside of you? Let it be the driving force for your business. All great mass movements that have ever happened have a charismatic leader behind.

Are you wondering how? Well, you just have to step into the role and play it right! Your audience and prospectors are looking for where to put their hope and be helped out of a difficult situation. People should see you as the expert, the voice they can listen to. To be this winning leader who will attract people around you, do the following:

Play as a charismatic leader and live the life your audience would like to live.

Show trust and certainty around your business.

You don't have to be born expert or great leader to attain this feat! But you should take time to familiarize yourself with your niche such that your audience can feel comfortable and be able to trust you. Remember that customers don't like to deal with starters or novices, so present yourself as an expert and serve your clients as such!

Don't appear boring!

Know how to be persuasive - encourage your audience to dream big, justify their failures, dispel their fears, confirm their suspicions and address them, take care of them, offer them a good quality-price ratio and help them identify themselves.

As a charismatic leader, your audience wants to know who you are, if you can be the solution to their problems. You must let them know what sets you apart from others. Who are you and what do you bring to the table? Take a stand and showcase your dream.

New Opportunity

The new opportunity is akin to the vehicle by which your audience will be moving in. This aspect of your mass movement push is very relevant to the message in this book. Every mass movement of the past rests on a new opportunity. You must have something new to offer your audience if you want to lead a mass movement to your passive income business.

Depending on your point of view, you may have admiration for individuals such as Gandhi or Mother Teresa and view them as outstanding, charismatic or attractive leaders. Each of these personalities had something new to offer to their followers to attract such a large audience around them. It's the power of attraction! People want to do things differently, give them the reason to follow you, prove to them that you really have what they are looking for.

At first, you need to design the new opportunity you're offering to your customers based on their needs. You then need to reassure them that your solution works better than all the other alternatives they may have and that it is the one they've long waited for. If your message is delivered correctly, your audience will not hesitate to come after you in great numbers.

When Steve Jobs launched his Inner Circle training program, which was designed to make great entrepreneurs; his attractive character, the solution he was offering, along with the new approach he was introducing, made the project such a successful one, until they could no longer contain the number of pending registrations to the program.

All three features are imperative. Many people tend to overlook the attractive character aspect. This is a huge mistake because, in addition to having an impact on your audience, it is through the attractive character aspect that you develop yourself into a charismatic entrepreneur!

Become an attractive character in front of your audience, not the other way round. That is your role as an entrepreneur. You are not expected to know everything in order to start. You get better by doing.

If you are the owner of a brick-and-mortar establishment, the first opportunity to grab your customers' attention is your storefront, your shop window; even the colors, are as much factors that help give your business the "wow factor" you need to attract consumers.

Unfortunately, this may be the make-or-break moment for a prospective buyer to set foot in your business, and if you don't have the right combination, you may miss out on the potential income. True! It is not always possible for a person to judge a book by its cover, but there is a valid reason why it is also said that first impressions are very important!

Try to consider the factors mentioned above as components representing the image of your establishment. What is the picture of your store? Whether it's trendy, kitschy, high-end, fun, creative, homey, etc., your picture is your own making, you are what it is and it's up to you to design it the right way.

The important point to keep in mind is that all of these factors must work together to create a brilliant first impression.

Here's a list of various ways to make your store more inviting, unforgettable and able to consistently drive mass movements:

Try not to be too loud in your designs

They say less is more, and that's exactly right when it comes to your business' display windows. Be simple yet clear with the design of your website. Allow for intuitiveness. Users should not be lost when accessing your website. Examine specifically different display ideas and determine the best atmosphere for you and your image. Make sure your display has a plan - a cluttered window will likely attract the curious, but not necessarily the eyes of the consumer.

Make sure you're selling your merchandise

Don't get lost in the glamor of your digital image that your prospective customers forget what you're precisely selling. Indicate clearly the goods and services you are offering through your business and use your image to promote, not to distract.

Show the best sides of your products

As an example, for a brick-and-mortar business, to make your products as attractive as possible, not only do you need adequate lighting for the window, entrance and facility, but you also need to ensure that your routine maintenance is at par.

Investing in cleaning equipment suited to your business is an absolute necessity to create and maintain the image you want to sell to your customers. This analogy applies appropriately to online entrepreneurs and their businesses.

Build and increase the attractiveness of your products

It is essential to position your products well to attract mass movement towards what you are offering for sale, this is an open door for increased sales. Do not underestimate this! You want your business to be a place frequented by people who say, "Oh, I have to stop there!" Use the magnetic attraction of strategically placed items, paying close attention to important aspects such as color, shape, etc. You want to attract attention by staying well organized with the display of your product.

Have fun with your products

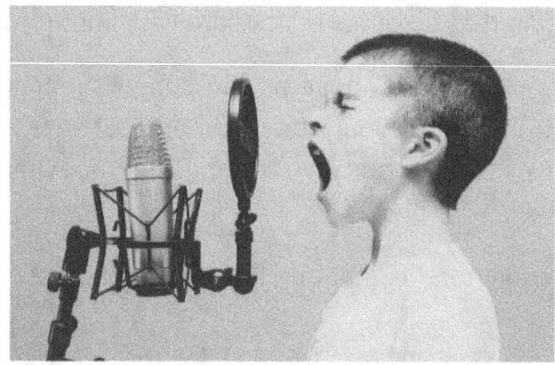

The use of cinemagraph may better showcase your products. If so, have fun with the setup. Use them to create poses indicating motion and activity. Your customers will find it both fun and helpful to discover how your products will actually look in real life.

Unsure where to get started from? Here's a list of wonderful steps to launch cinemagraph display concepts.

Use your creative genius

You have your cinemagraph; let your creative spirit express itself! Experiment with colors and patterns to accentuate the product you are trying to convey as well as the overall purpose of the message.

Customers prefer to deal with businesses that are able to offer them something unique. Keep this in mind when building your store's shopping experience.

Don't lose your goal or theme

Although creativity is a great tool, if you do not continually revisit your basic message and image you are presenting to potential customers, you may find yourself far off. If this should happen, you should go back to your basic idea while keeping things in their simplicity. If you maintain this mentality and combine it with pleasure and creativity, you're on your way to a winning combination.

Roll out the welcome mat

Make sure that your customers understand that you are accessible and that you want them to be there too. Welcome them with an awesomely greeting mat, a relaxed backdrop or scintillating music. Appeal to their senses, and they will soon thank you for your efforts.

Make sure that your inventory is prepared to manage promoted or featured products.

Do some research to find out more about your demographics and market before selecting your featured image. This will help you design your image around the items that your region will most likely need, as well as build an inventory sufficient for the actual sale.

So, build your store while focusing on your customer base. Keep in mind the potential customers in your area and find a featured picture that fits this demography.

You are bound to boost your traffic in no time with the right products and pictures and eventually enjoy the fruits of your labor. Remember to often review your ideas to keep your store image fresh. With more sales and more revenue, the time spent will surely pay off and you will be glad to feel that impression of personal accomplishment.

Get Your Communication on board

The lack of effective communication between your teams can create a major obstacle in the execution of your business.

Develop internal communication systems, whether it's team meetings, video conferencing or emails. For instance, if you are running a retail store and you really want to be hyper-organized, you can use retail communication tools to streamline communication as well as manage tasks across your entire business.

Set to win fresh customers?

How to attract new customers:

1. Get down-and-dirty to find your ideal customers

Most business owners are too scattered in their targets. Far too many entrepreneurs fail because they try to be too many things at once. If you are too broad and you are trying to attract everyone, you end up not appealing to anyone. You have to go back to the basics and identify your ideal customer base to generate serious leads. Define their type of demographics, industry, personality, and emotions. Identify and target a specific type of individuals.

2. Solve Problems

People have problems, we all do! These are solved by great businesses. Unfortunately, there are so many superficial marketing messages on the Internet. Generic tweets, blog posts and shares are used by many! Never generate such mediocre content! Instead, your marketing message must stand out from the crowd. You can't disregard your genuine customers by writing less focused blog posts or emails. As an entrepreneur, you have the expertise and the answers to a particular set of issues, hence your marketing content must precisely demonstrate how they are solved.

3. Be bold

There's a ton of boring content in the world, so to make people fall in love with you, make sure that yours sparks interest!

Like a virtual dump, you should throw away all the boring stuff! Use everyday language while staying distinct in your message. Make sure to "zag" when everyone else "zigs". And get rid of corporate voice, buzzwords, passive voice and bring out the distinct character in you.

You may think that sounding important is good for your business, or maybe that's what you learned in college! But the reality is that by taking this approach, you sound boring and mediocre, like so many other entrepreneurs out there! This makes your content look so uninteresting and unable to meet the expectations of your prospects. Make your voice special instead but do not try to be someone else!

The secret "ingredient" that distinguishes your business from the rest is your genuine brand personality. Develop your personality such that people feel amplified and valued whenever they are dealing with you. Show them the real you.

4. Relate to your audience with your storytelling skills

Take advantage of the power of storytelling to reach out to your ideal customers.

Storytelling has been a unifying element for people since ancient times. Our brains are wired to be story processors regardless of the location. An ancestral elder can tell a captivating story next to a campfire explaining how zebras got their stripes or Peter Pan can be read out by a parent to catch their child's attention! Storytelling evokes a powerful neurological reaction! Stories stick faster in our memories.

This implies that in your marketing material, you must be able to tell your story in order to get your audience to relate to you. This will also give them the reason to do business with you and drive your ideal customers towards you.

Entrepreneurs who are making it, do take advantage of the power of storytelling to reach out to their ideal clients. Here's an example:

Jenna has built a great blogging business around her story: She lived from paycheck to paycheck, with lots of debt, she eventually started to feel her dreams fading away. Knowing that she had to make a radical change, she swapped for an unpredictable adventure, renouncing the stability of a full-time job and stepping out of her comfort zone. And so, Tiny House Giant Journey was born, building a small house on wheels to travel the globe... She is a fierce ambassador of the small house movement and constantly finds intelligent methods to make the most out of a small living space. She has now visited many countries around the world, enjoying her financial freedom and describing herself as a full-time happiness addict. Through her storytelling, many people identify with her and do not hesitate to join her community of followers and be part of her list of potential customers.

The more members you acquire, the more traffic you will have, which will generate more revenue for your business. Instead of churning out enormous amounts of blog posts and emails, focus on regular quality messages. Tell your story! Be authentic! Inspire people! Solve problems! You will eventually start receiving calls and emails from people who want to use your product or use your services.

Secret 6: Why Is College Teaching Irrelevant in Today's Market for Entrepreneurs?

It has been observed that business schools have little need to worry about the added value for the end user - the students. The inherent MBA learning is less important than the high-salaried job-offers it provides. What a business school teaches hardly matters in the current configuration.

There are many governments, private organizations and foundations worldwide offering business and management education. But most of these business schools are faced with crisis of irrelevance. They are in an incredible race to the bottom! It is not even clear what an MBA consists of anymore! There is a lack of quality and consistency in the growth of general leadership knowledge. Incentives are based more on research and academic credibility, not really on understanding and practice of leadership!

Colleges teach and encourage students to always be innovative, to start something new! You learn how to get a loan to start a business and methods to help you break-even; which for most starters can take up to 6 years, if you are lucky and depending on the nature and magnitude of your business! You are taught how to sell your business as soon as you start having sufficient cash flow and encouraged to re-invent each time, thus repeating the cycle of working for venture capitalists lending you the money!

Don't re-invent the wheel! Many online entrepreneurs are failing, and their websites are dead because of this! You don't need to be a genius creator! Be a detective!

Contrary to college teachings, here is the ideal process used by successful online entrepreneurs:

Sub-market choice

Select your core market among the three human strong desires: Health, Wealth and Relationship. Recall that the needs of humans fall in these three categories. By approaching your market with these in mind, you're on the hot selling ground that will quickly have an impact. Carve out a niche for yourself in this ecosystem.

Then select your sub-market or niche. Will the sub-market you have chosen meet the needs of your potential customers? Define your dream customers and specify their problems and the required solutions. Prepare your products or services that will be able to solve those problems. Work out your core offer that sells your products or services. Launch your marketing and sales campaign, tweak and relaunch until you get it right.

Schools teach "understanding," but in life, wisdom is much more needed. "Never mistake wisdom for understanding. One helps you make a living; the other helps you make a life. "— Sandra Carey. Instead of equipping children with essential life skills such as money management, negotiation, communication, and so on, schools mainly teach subjects full of data to memorize.

Since college is meant to prepare for professional life, why should real-life situations be left out. Reports suggest that many graduates do not feel prepared for work or business when they finish college and find themselves in jobs they never really wanted to do.

Training programs are nowadays in vogue! This is a valid evidence of the inadequacy of the traditional model of education. In 1 to 3 months of training, these bootcamps produce entrepreneurs capable of achieving monthly income in excess of what they could ever earn in an entire year in their conventional jobs.

These training programs include workshops tailored to real-life scenarios and deliver results that are far better than the four years of typical academic training; not to mention the long months or years of painful and frustrating waiting period between college exit and the moment you actually find employment.

More secrets not taught in college for entrepreneurs!

List building

Why is list building considered as the real asset on internet for online businesses?

Regarded as the backbone of any business, list building impacts the following:

3 Types of traffic

Identify who are your dream customers and where they hang out. Which congregation or group are they members?

Type #1: Traffic that you can control: For instance, Facebook owns its traffic but allows you to regulate certain types of it via paid advertising. The same analogy works for other platforms such as Google ads or Instagram and so on. You can then import the traffic that you are able to control and customize it by making it your own. This is paid traffic!

Type #2: Traffic that you earn: This is where you make use of techniques such as SEO or Search Engine Optimization, allowing you to build your list from your blogs for instance. You can acquire this type of traffic through the creation and entertainment of a Facebook group. But as an entrepreneur, you have to account for your time and energy invested in building your list this way. This traffic is also called organic traffic. This is relatively free traffic!

Type #3: Traffic that you own: Whether you're getting paid or organic traffic, you're going to own that traffic ultimately. This is the list that is completely under your control, you decide when and how to use it for your product or service promotions or for your sales campaigns. This is ultimately your real asset on internet as an entrepreneur or marketer.

Your list will determine how much money you can earn each month. According to my good friend and mentor, Russell Brunson, the mastermind of the innovative One Funnel Away Challenge, CEO of Clickfunnels and sales funnels pioneer, the minimum income you can generate from your list that you already own is $ 1 per contact per month in direct marketing business.

So, for instance, if your estimated financial freedom is $ 10,000 per month, then to achieve that, you need to create a list of at least 10,000 contacts in your direct marketing business.

All the contacts in your list are all yours to promote to for FREE! You can send them advertising messages without incurring any ads costs.

Hence the list is the real asset of your business, whatever its nature!

Explore more valuable resources and author's recommendations here: **www.andymutambya.com**

Secret 7: What Is That Vehicle or Platform That Will Turn You into That Money-Making Machine?

This is the system that allows you to deliver your offer.

A lot of websites are dead because they are hosted on wrong platforms. Making the right choice of system is so crucial to the success of your business that you will not even need to convince anyone to do business with you; This is the work of your platform!

You need the best system that works for you as the best sales and marketing agent that has ever existed! A platform that can bring you the desired income day and night! A program that gives you financial, temporal and geographical independence, hence allowing you to spend more time with your loved ones. You'll no longer need to trade your time for money!

Businesses and Matching Platforms

For every business type, there is a platform that is best suited. Find the right one for your business.

Affiliate Marketing

Most online marketing websites intended to generate passive income are dying at launch! Why? One of the main reasons is due to inappropriate platforms on which they are hosted.

For instance, affiliate marketers are among those badly hit for wrong choice of platform!

Affiliate marketing can be described as a method of earning commissions for referring products or services from one company to other businesses or individuals. You can discover a particular product or service and decide to promote it; usually from your own blog. You will then receive profits or commissions for each sale you make. These are essentially online marketing references.

A company will create a program that pays fees for the traffic or revenues they produce through external websites or people.

This enables internet consumers, influencers and online entrepreneurs to earn cash for promoting other people's businesses, products or services.

For instance:

Blogging

As popular as blogging is today, most blogging websites are dead as a result of the unsupportive content management system.

Initially, blogging began as a result of a private internet log in which an individual would report about their day. The word "blog" originated from "internet log." Like most new internet technologies, many entrepreneurs saw the marketing potential and business blogging took off from there. Not only can a blog be used for marketing purposes, but it can also be in itself a home-based business.

Here is a brief description of a blog, why it is famous, and tips for launching your own.

Many individuals are confused about what makes up a website blog. Part of the issue is that many entrepreneurs use both interchangeably. But a blog has two particular characteristics that distinguish it from a traditional website.

• Blogs are often updated. Whether it's a mother's blog sharing her parenting adventures, a culinary blog on new recipes, or a company sharing their facilities updates, blogs have fresh content added on a regular basis. Websites may sometimes have fresh data, but most of the data they provide is static.

• Blogs allow the involvement of readers. Blogs are often valuable because of the readers' ability to comment and talk to the blogger and other blog readers. Previously, websites had guest logs where users could signal that they had visited, but a blog allows for discussion and more interaction than a traditional website.

What are the preferred platforms for your business model? Of course, when it comes to blogging, long-term content management systems are not far off!

Currently, WordPress ranks as the best content management platform. You can use the self-hosted WordPress platform that gives you total control of the system. Blogger is another platform from Google but WordPress remains the most reliable and user-friendly.

Social Media Marketing

Social media marketing is currently a hot field that successful online entrepreneurs are taking advantage of. There are so many of them out there at the moment such as:

- Facebook
- YouTube
- Twitter
- LinkedIn
- Instagram
- WhatsApp
- Pinterest

There are many methods to promote your business by using paid social marketing, and each channel has its own set of paid advertising alternatives.

Take Facebook for instance.

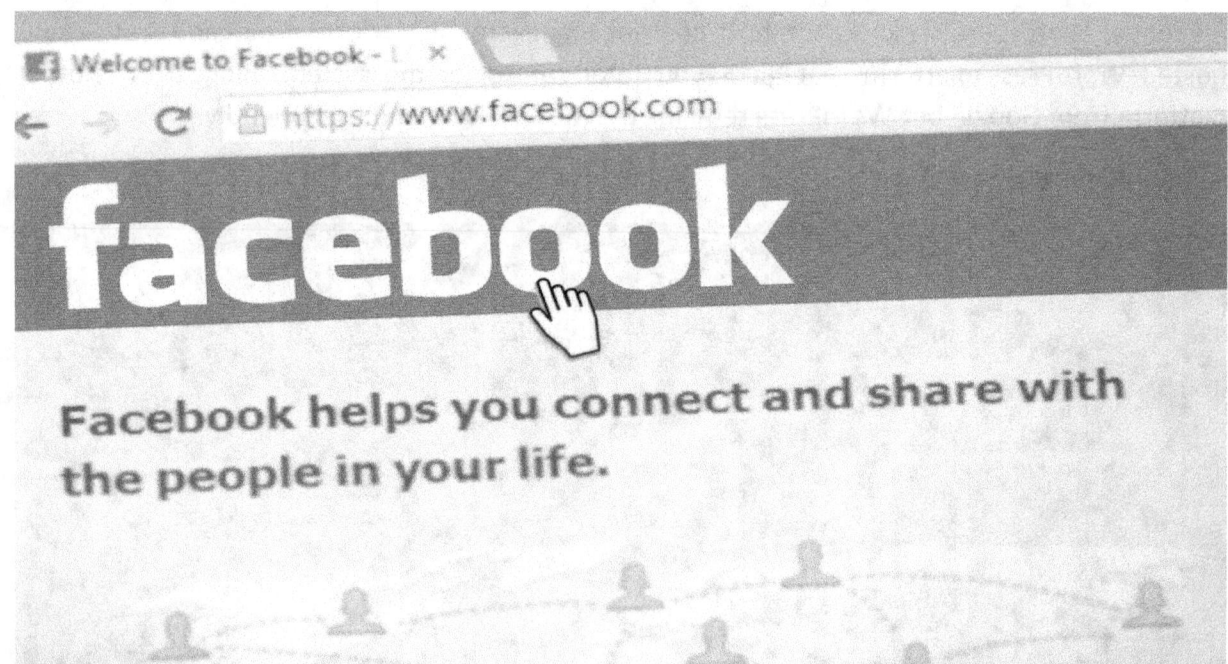

To boost your publications, you can pay or generate a dedicated Facebook ad through a marketing campaign tailored to your objectives.

Most paid ads on social networks are also called "pay per click". Shopping for goods and services is one of the top 10 reasons why people use social media nowadays.

Social media advertising is one of the two major types of digital marketing you should be doing on social networking sites. The other is the management of social media.

When done correctly, advertising on social networks allows you to advertise to your customers in a way that they really appreciate. You avoid forcing people to see your ads when they don't wish to.

Email Marketing

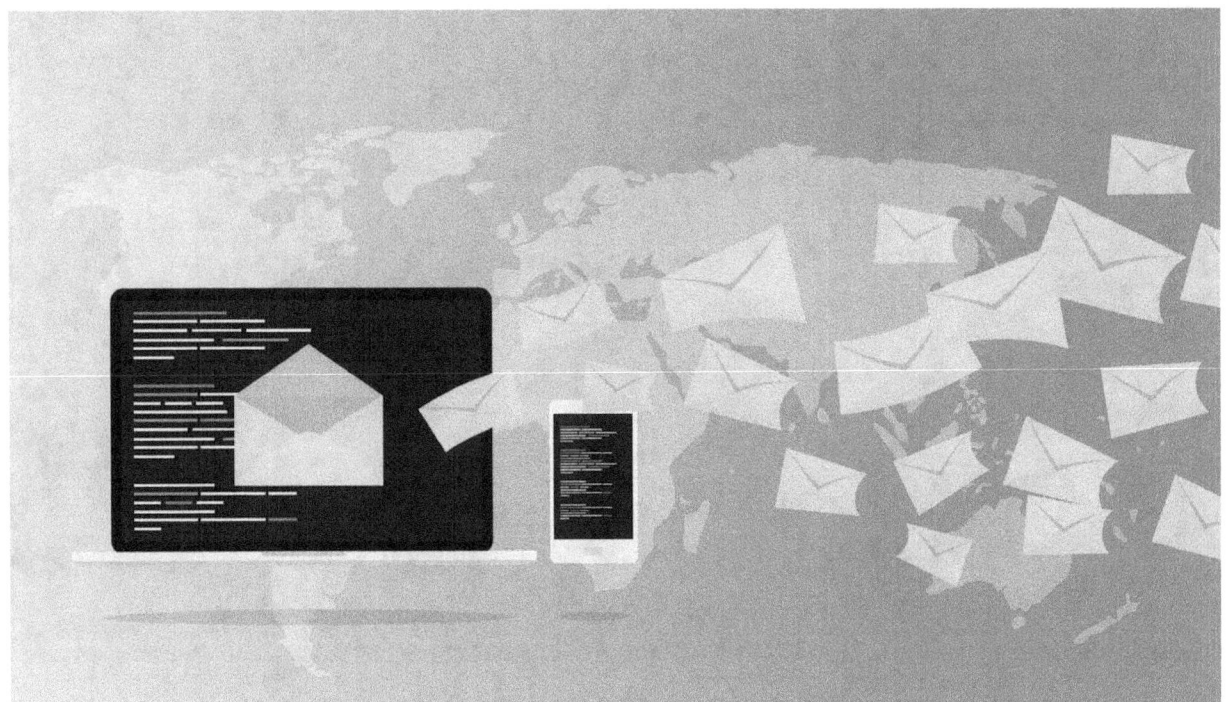

Email marketing has been, for a long time, the cornerstone of any business seeking to generate revenue online. Your websites are dead if you cannot connect and interact with your customers. It offers immediate customer contact and allows you to get potential customers to visit your website.

You can provide your clients with updates, interesting news, reminders, etc. in a matter of minutes and in a few easy steps. At the same time, you can use newsletters as printable elements of e-mail marketing. Send customizable messages that look realistic and represent your business the way you want.

People want brands that they can trust, businesses that understand them! Personalized, customized and appropriate emails are a better way to provide information tailored to their needs and preferences.

E-commerce and Dropshipping

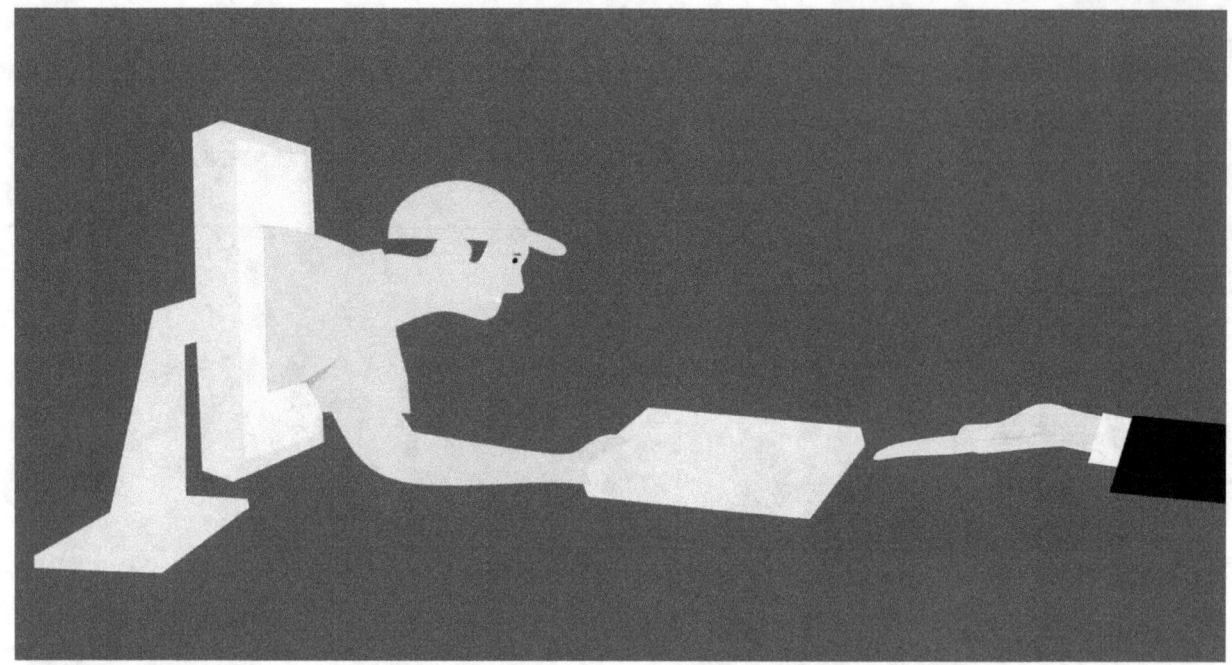

E-commerce is an important player in today's online business model. At the moment, many entrepreneurs are in this category. Here are some of the notable platforms that most online entrepreneurs use for their e-commerce businesses.

1. Shopify

This is a Canadian-based e-commerce solution. Shopify has helped global internet companies with a strong focus on social marketing and mobile shopping. Founded in 2004, Shopify has always kept pace with changing e-commerce trends and techniques, breaking ground with strong additions like social shopping where your clients never leave their social media platform to purchase from you.

The Good Part: You can directly integrate Shopify into your Facebook account for $ 9 and turn it into an e-commerce store.

The Downside: Even with all the aforementioned benefits of Shopify, the platform has some disadvantages. One of the major disadvantages is the additional transaction fees that you must pay if you do not use the Shopify Payment facility. In addition, many useful and practical extensions require additional investments. Perhaps the most difficult is Shopify's "own coding" language, which forces e-commerce store owners to pay an additional cost of customization.

Early-stage entrepreneurs who need a standard e-commerce solution can take advantage of Shopify platform. It's simple to use and you can easily start your e-commerce business in no time. Depending on your demands and budget, you can choose from Shopify packages ranging from $ 29 to $ 299 a month.

2. Magento:

Released in March 2008, Magento is a website platform for open source e-commerce. It has become one of the most common e-commerce platforms on the market due to its reliability and scalability. Lots of prominent names like Burger King, Pepe Jeans, and Liverpool F.C. are on Magento.

The Downside: The use of Magento isn't for everyone, especially if you're not a programmer or if you don't have the support of programmers around you. And then comes the price tag; the basic version is free but having a business version implies shelling out at least $20,000/year. If you do not have personnel programmers, be ready to invest in programming expenses for third parties as well.

Magento is the ideal option for enterprise-level internet stores with a huge number of products. Due to its complex configuration, its cost and its extremely technical management requirements, it is not recommended for small businesses.

3. YoKart

Specially designed for startups and small and medium-sized businesses or SMBs, YoKart is a turnkey solution with a wealthy e-commerce marketplace solution for building multi-seller shops like Amazon, eBay, and Etsy. While a multi-vendor version is available on many other e-commerce platforms, YoKart is specialized in this specific sector. YoKart now offers an even larger solution with its recent upgrade (YoKart V8). Its multilingual and multi-currency features allow store owners to expand their reach around the world. It also incorporates many payment gateways, an integrated analytics tool, rewards and discount coupon management features.

The good part: In addition to a lifetime license, the market owner receives the source code of the website.

The Downside: YoKart has some disadvantages; because of the solid framework, a developer with comprehensive PHP expertise will be required to customize YoKart. Plus, it's not like the open source Magento. The default topics are available in the Startup and GoQuick Packages. And unlike Magento, YoKart focuses primarily on SMBs, which means that the required features are already available in the classic packages. Customization would be a must for large-scale businesses.

SMBs can take full advantage of YoKart. The $ 250 start package is the most affordable. This is a pragmatic technique to test the viability of your business model. Once you are sure of your business, you can then easily upgrade to greater variants such as GoQuick, GoCustom Lite and GoCustom.

4. BigCommerce

BigCommerce has grown to more than 55,000 online stores since its inception and is recognized as one of the most prominent providers of e-commerce software. From renowned companies like Martha Stewart & Toyota to many small and medium-sized enterprises, BigCommerce helps companies of all sizes to launch their internet storefronts. The extensive list of built-in features of BigCommerce is very useful for e-commerce entrepreneurs who lack fundamental coding capabilities.

The Bad Part: For those who want to begin a multi-seller shop like the Amazon platform, they may discover that some of the other e-commerce platforms offer much more integrated marketplace models. The lack of enough free themes may be another problem with BigCommerce. This software lags behind other e-commerce platforms with only 7 free themes, when most program offer more than 20. But that doesn't alter the fact that you get a lot of premium themes and plenty of customization choices to offer a distinctive identity to your business.

BigCommerce is an ideal solution for e-commerce entrepreneurs who want a full-fledged store without the problems of coding, plug-in integration issues and other technical hurdles. If you can settle for a tiny selection of free themes or if you want to expand on a premium theme, BigCommerce is the solution for your e-commerce platform.

5. VTEX

It is a Brazilian cloud-based application which achieved a gross turnover of $ 1.8 billion in 2016. Among the major global players, there are local business chains, such as Wal-Mart, Whirlpool, Coca-Cola, Sony, L'Oréal, Lego, Staples, and many more.

The Good Part: The Password Free Checkout is a notable factor that differentiates VTEX from the rest of the e-commerce line-ups. This particular feature is thought to increase organic traffic by 30%, increase revenue by 28% and increase conversion rates by a whopping 54%.

The Downside: Although the company claims that cloud-based e-commerce technology implements 68% faster than traditional configurations, VTex has a major disadvantage for online entrepreneurs wishing to keep control of their own storefront: it relies on the SaaS model, so you're really not going to have full ownership of your e-commerce store or source code.

VTEX and its boost in conversion rates can benefit businesses with a substantial amount of monthly transactions and an annual turnover of $1 million or more. However, because of higher costs, VTEX can be expensive for many SMBs

6. WooCommerce

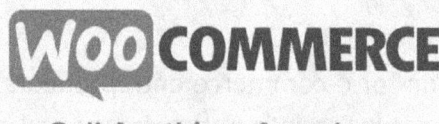

A free WordPress plugin, WooCommerce is a name that does not need to be introduced in the world of e-commerce. It comes with a secure portal for payment, a shopping cart and they both work very well! Open source and easy to use for WordPress enthusiasts, WooCommerce needs an additional plug-in to start an e-commerce store with multiple vendors.

The Disadvantages: the installation of WooCommerce is free, but an additional investment is needed to fully integrate the shopping cart into the system. Plus, you will not understand how to use WooCommerce until you first acquire sufficient WordPress expertise. But the biggest problem of WooCommerce is scalability. As your business grows and you have more and more suppliers, products, and customers in your database, WooCommerce starts to slow down.

If you want to stick to WordPress websites and do not anticipate having a big, high-volume online store, then WooCommerce is a feasible alternative for you.

7. Tictail

Tictail is more like a do it yourself or DIY marketplace where custom design, community integration, ease of use and overall e-commerce attractiveness are more focused. Fashion designers and distributors can set up their virtual store within a few minutes.

The Bad: The lack of payment processors, especially when other e-commerce platforms offer plenty of payment alternatives is a downside. Tictail is free to bring a commission from the global marketplace. However, the custom store frees you from paying extra fees to Tictail for every sale that takes place on the platform.

If you're considering going global, but you're not sure if your business model is going to succeed or not, Tictail is an excellent test run platform. It's not intended for larger businesses though!

Final Thoughts: An e-commerce platform is not a "one size fits all" solution for everyone. All the e-commerce platforms aforementioned are designed to meet various types of business needs. The curated list is intended to help you make calculated choice in your selection of the platform that best serves your requirements.

Various e-commerce platforms are selected based on business models and scales of operations.

Clearly, not all systems work in the same way, so it is essential to choose the right one.

The first thing to do is to know your business model. Indeed, each business model has its own platform that suits it best.

Imagine your own house under construction. Whether built by you or a contractor, you will be primarily concerned with design, layout, and other factors such as closet space, etc.

At another level, you'll also worry about materials, engineering and behind-the-scenes know-how, even if you do not know exactly how craftsmanship and everything else works together, you'd want to make sure the work is properly done so that you can end up with a sustainable home.

The same analogy works for online business platforms! Here are some questions to ask when choosing your business platform:

- *Is it well supported and frequently updated?*
- *Is the level of security a concern?*
- *Is it trustworthy?*
- *Is it SEO friendly?*
- *Will I rely on my designer?*
- *Do I have the right to use it 100%?*
- *Will it be user-friendly?*
- *Functionality: Will it perform exactly as expected?*
- *Can you update it easily? (You'd probably want to avoid proprietary content management systems and website builders).*
- *Do you need 24/7 support?*

Content Marketing

Why are so many entrepreneurs not exploiting the new powers of the internet? Websites are dead without content! Content rule in the world of internet!

It is reported that, on average, people use their phones 70 times a day to surf online, whether for fun, for learning or for shopping online. Therefore, as an online entrepreneur, you should build your content with those three aspects in mind while paying attention to whether you are selling health, wealth or relationships in order to meet your audience needs.

Remember! It's all about providing added value!

Author's recommendations and other helpful details can be accessed at www.andymutambya.com.

Conclusion

There is definitely a reason why your websites are dead! The 7 secrets examined above should bring your business back to life.

Model those who are succeeding. Your passive income websites may have died because you continue to stick to what you have always known. It's not your opinion that counts but the market demand!

The secret about the ethical hacking of your influencer is not about copying the superficial appearances of their web pages, but it lies in the modeling of their platforms and, more importantly, in the modeling of their marketing messages, thus hook, story and offer!

Remember that customers can buy the same products at different prices simply because they are packaged or grouped differently, and therefore offered in different ways.

The dangerous approach of college or university education of pushing people to always be innovative is one of the main reasons for the failure of many online entrepreneurs.

By acting solely on new creations, as an entrepreneur, you are mostly faced with cold traffic. Meaning that, after you have invested your time, energy, money, and other resources to deliver your incredible innovation, you will always have the responsibility to inform your potential customers of their own problems, then try to convince them about your suggested solutions that you think they might require. As an entrepreneur, you will face a huge challenge in the current market since your potential customers will not allow you more than 7 seconds to impress them by giving them a reason to move on to the next step towards the conclusion of a sale.

Successful entrepreneurs, online or offline, do not care much about reinventing the wheel, but are turning themselves into money making machines by smartly hacking their influencers and applying all the 7 secrets examined here.

If someone cannot make you money, then they do not deserve yours!

These top 7 weird secrets are bound to increasing your traffic, conversions, and sales while helping you boost your business and ultimately improve your life!

To evaluate and understand how your advertising investment converts and if it generates money for you, you need to use DIRECT RESPONSE MARKETING!

So, how do you make money online in the most profitable way? The approach is not to immediately withdraw your profits; identify your ads that are converting, boost your budget on them, i.e. reinvest your profit back on them by rolling them 8 to 10 times until you reach a point of ad fatigue.

These top 7 weird secrets reveal how to make money online! By leveraging the power of the internet as disclosed here, many entrepreneurs are turning into money making machines!

It is often said that knowledge is power; but if you acquire knowledge and do not act, you have nothing! Take action now and grow your business by visiting these sites recommended by the author: https://ofachallenge01.passiveincomeideas-foryou.com/optintbdmbi8x, https://affiliateprogramsforbeginners.com/, http://jobsrendezvous.com/ and www.andymutambya.com.

www.ingramcontent.com/pod-product-compliance
Lightning Source LLC
Chambersburg PA
CBHW080850220526
45467CB00008B/2454